THE POETRY OF
ABRAHAM COWLEY

David Trotter

ROWMAN AND LITTLEFIELD
Totowa, New Jersey

PR
3374
T7
1979

First published in the United States 1979
By Rowman and Littlefield, Totowa, N.J.

Library of Congress Cataloging in Publication Data
Trotter, David, 1951–
  The poetry of Abraham Cowley.

  Based on the author's thesis, Cambridge, 1975.
  Bibliography: p.
  Includes index.
  1. Cowley, Abraham, 1618–1667—Criticism and
  interpretation.   I. Title.
PR3374.T7   1979   821'.4   78–31613
ISBN 0–8476–6157–1

Printed in Great Britain

For my parents

Contents

List of Abbreviations

COWLEY'S WORKS

P   *Poems*, A. R. Waller (ed.) (Cambridge, 1905)
W   *Works* (1668)

References to these works are included in the text.

PERIODICALS

HLQ   *Huntington Library Quarterly*
JEGP   *Journal of English and Germanic Philology*
MLN   *Modern Language Notes*
MLR   *Modern Language Review*
MP   *Modern Philology*
NQ   *Notes and Queries*
PMLA   *Publications of the Modern Language Association of America*
PQ   *Philological Quarterly*
RES   *Review of English Studies*
SB   *Studies in Bibliography*
SEL   *Studies in English Literature, 1500–1900*
SP   *Studies in Philology*
TLS   *Times Literary Supplement*

All books cited in this study were published in London, unless otherwise stated.

1 Introduction

Literary criticism tells us that nothing very much happened between Donne and Dryden. Apart, that is, from a Revolution and the slow pondering of an epic poem to rival Homer and Virgil and Dante. It tells us that there were striking individual voices but no specifiable practices of writing, no equivalent to a 'Metaphysical' or an 'Augustan' poetic. Those practices of writing we *can* specify have on the whole had to be defined by what they are not: by the extent to which they reveal the decadence of a 'Metaphysical' mode or the seeds of 'Augustanism'. Criticism has not allowed them any positively defining characteristics, for the focus of its analysis is always elsewhere, as the titles of studies covering the period demonstrate: *From Donne to Dryden: The Revolt against Metaphysical Poetry, Metaphysical to Augustan, Towards an Augustan Poetic, The School of Donne, The Heirs of Donne and Jonson, From Concord to Dissent*. The first of these studies was published in 1940, the last in 1973, but the terms of definition consistently direct us elsewhere: school of, heirs of, revolt against, towards.

We shall go on thinking of the middle years of the century as a lethargy between organised initiatives until we find positive rather than negative terms of definition for the vagrant forms of literary life they did harbour. One move in this direction has led to an exact historicist reading of the poetry of the period.[1] Placed in a historical context rather than in literary tradition, the enigmatic code of its allusions deciphered, the poem will supposedly come into its own. Such historicist readings have, in some cases, been conducted brilliantly and proved indispensable to our appreciation of seventeenth-century poetry; I shall myself employ this method on occasion (for example, in my discussion of Book IV of the *Davideis*). But there is a constant danger that these readings will repeat the mistake of their style-orientated competitors:

1

namely, to locate the 'significance' of the text they are examining *elsewhere*. Too often the text remains symptomatic (of 'history', this time, rather than of 'Metaphysical' or 'Augustan' style); the fierce light of reality shines elsewhere, from political pamphlets or from 'A Valediction: Forbidding Mourning', and is palely reflected on the wall of the poem in question. The terms of definition, in other words, are still negative, for all their promise of specificity.

The solution, surely, is to allow for the relative autonomy of various 'levels' of activity, each of which has its own time and history; and for the uneven development of those 'levels'. Rather than assuming that literature is either independent of, or dependent on, history—the two views summarised above—we can study the specific history of groupings of discursive practices; a history which relates to, but does not owe its truth to, other histories. We are not pursuing the history of ideas, but the history of the conditions of thought: of what makes it possible to think in a certain way at one time, and in an entirely different way at another. I want to explain how a mode of thinking and speaking which had held a marginal position became dominant and began to favour a different range of statement. Most historians would agree that the seventeenth century witnessed, in Britain at least, an 'intellectual revolution', although the pace and extent and significance of this 'revolution' remain matters of contention; rationalist philosophy and the 'rise of science' are usually cited as the major catalysts of change.[2] But if we are to understand how the 'intellectual revolution' invalidated one range of statement and made another possible, in literature as well as in science and philosophy, then we must define it as a change in the conditions of thought; we cannot rely on the terms provided by the history of ideas. We must be able to talk about a change which occurred more or less simultaneously across various disciplines: philosophy, science, rhetoric, legal practice, literature, religious doctrine. I believe that the terms for such a discussion can be found in the work of Thomas Hobbes, which, during the period between 1640 and 1651, was persistently concerned with the feasibility of changing the very conditions of thought. Hobbes's treatise on· *Human Nature*, published in 1650 but circulated in manuscript as part of *The Elements of Law* in 1640, made an important distinction between two discursive practices, between speaking the truth on one hand and providing evidence of the truth on the other:

What *truth* is, hath been defined in the precedent chapter; what *evidence* is, I *now* set down: and it is the concomitance of a man's *conception* with the *words* that signify such conception in the act of ratiocination: for when a man reasoneth with his lips only, to which the mind suggesteth only the beginning, and followeth not the words of his mouth with the conceptions of his mind, out of custom of so speaking; though he begin his ratiocination with true propositions, and proceed with certain syllogisms, and thereby make always true conclusions; yet are not his conclusions *evident* to him, for want of the *concomitance of conception* with his words: for if the words alone were sufficient, a *parrot* might be taught as well to know truth, as to speak it. Evidence is to truth, as the sap to the tree, which, so far as it creepeth along with the body and branches, keepeth them alive; where it forsaketh them, they die: for this evidence, which is meaning with our words, is the life of truth.

This is not, I think, just another attack on empty eloquence; Hobbes was writing at a time when the divisions between King and Parliament were deepening, and when the 'custom of so speaking' was in the most general sense under threat. Hobbes's response to this threat is to distinguish between a merely spoken truth, 'when a man reasoneth with his lips only', and a truth that is known by the self-evident concomitance of word and concept, without reference to the way in which it is spoken. Hobbes developed this distinction in *De Cive* (1642), where he argued that the reasons why we accept a proposition as true derive 'either from the *proposition itself*, or from the *person propounding*'. In the first instance, we recognise a concomitance between word and concept, and the 'assent which we give, is called *knowledge* or *science*'; in the second instance, we consider the speaker 'so learned that he is not deceived, and we see no reason why he should deceive us', and our assent, 'because it grows not from any confidence of our own, but from another man's knowledge, is called *faith*'. Science and faith are familiar enough protagonists, but the value of Hobbes's account lies in his readiness to define them as different customs of thinking and speaking (different discursive practices), each of which has its own rules and procedures. One operates by allusion to tradition, by restating what has always been taken to be the case; the other by self-effacing presentation of the facts. Hobbes returned to the subject in *Leviathan* (1651), arguing that:

when we believe any saying whatsoever it be, to be true, from arguments taken, not from the thing itself, or from the principles of natural reason, but from the authority, and good opinion we have, of him that hath said it; then is the speaker, or person we believe in, or trust in, and whose word we take, the object of our faith; and the honour done in believing, is done to him only. And consequently, when we believe that the Scriptures are the word of God, having no immediate revelation from God himself, our belief, faith, and trust is in the church; whose word we take, and acquiesce therein. And they that believe that which a prophet relates unto them in the name of God, take the word of the prophet, do honour to him, and in him trust, and believe, touching the truth of what he relateth, whether he be a true, or a false prophet. And so it is with all other history . . . If *Livy* say the Gods made once a cow speak, and we believe it not; we distrust not God therein, but *Livy*. So that it is evident, that whatsoever we believe, upon no other reason, than what is drawn from authority of men only, and their writings; whether they be sent from God or not, is faith in men only.[3]

I shall term arguments taken from 'the thing itself, or from the principles of natural reason', *propositional truth*; and arguments taken from 'the authority, and good opinion we have, of him that hath said it', *locutionary truth*.[4] I want to distinguish between a method of argument which claims that a statement should be judged on its own merits, without reference to the way it is made or has been made before; and a method which depends for its effect on the way a statement is made or has been made before, which relies on convincing the addressee that anything said in this way must be true. The exponent of locutionary truth relies on the existence of a code which has always in the past rendered intelligible the kind of proposition he wants to put forward; the prophet, in Hobbes's example, will try to act as prophets always have, according to the code which has always governed the behaviour and speech of prophets in the past. Each message he utters will convince not in itself but by the way it reinvents that code. The exponent of propositional truth, on the other hand, is suspicious of codes, those emblems of subservience to tradition; he does not want us to believe what he says simply because such things have always been said in that way and always proved true in the past. His messages are apparently without origin, apparently uncoded;

we are invited to apply the principles of 'natural reason' and judge them strictly according to their own merits. The *Leviathan* acknowledges both methods of argument and therefore includes two structures of political authority. The commonwealth described in Books I and II relies on the procedures of propositional truth, the 'Christian Commonwealth' of Book III on the procedures of locutionary truth. But the 'intellectual revolution' involved the switching of the method of propositional truth from a subordinate to a dominant position across various disciplines, and the relative downgrading of its rival.

I believe that this historical process left its mark more plainly on the poetry of Abraham Cowley than on the work of any other contemporary writer. Cowley was only too aware of the pressures exerted on a writer during a period of violent upheaval; as he put it, 'a warlike, various, and a tragical age is best to *write of*, but worst to *write in*' (P, 7). Yet history penetrated the 'form' rather than the 'content' of his work. It is not so much that he felt obliged to make statements the truth of which must be read off against what was actually said and done at the time, although he certainly did; but rather that he found modes of statement becoming impossible, so to speak, as he used them. Established modes of statement reached a limit, moved into conflict with each other, failed to contain proliferating rhetorics or tones of voice; other modes emerged to replace them. My intention is to approach the 1656 edition of Cowley's *Poems* as a 'limit text': as the place where one discursive practice finds its historical limit and another begins to establish itself. The 1656 *Poems* assembles all of his major poems to date, excluding juvenilia and the suppressed *Civil War*. It contains four sections: occasional verse, including the elegy 'On the Death of Mr. Crashaw', love-lyrics (*The Mistress*), Pindaric odes and an unfinished epic, the *Davideis*. The collection was the most varied and most ambitious of its time; it was also, as Cowley's Preface made clear, trapped in the aftermath of civil war. Cowley subsequently published *Verses written on several occasions* (1663), which was included in the posthumous edition of his *Works* (1668) together with 'Several Discourses by way of Essays in Verse and Prose'. Some of this later work may have been more accomplished than anything in the 1656 *Poems*, but it was firmly embedded in a cultural consensus and thus able to ignore the problems which made the earlier collection such an imposing articulation of a specific historical process. I have not referred widely outside the

1656 *Poems*, to Cowley's subsequent writings or to other contemporary poets, because I thought the argument to be sufficiently complex already and worth stating in the purest condition possible.

There is a history which informs what has usually been termed the 'content' of a poem; and another—related but not dependent—history which occupies what has usually been termed its 'form'. This study will concern itself with the latter and will not on the whole attempt to relate the specific history of discursive practices to other histories (political, economic, social). I do not wish to deprecate the study of these other histories, but I felt that in the present state of the art a method which isolated would prove more valuable than one which synthesised. A certain crudeness has resulted from this determination to offer emphatic terms of argument (and devil take the hindmost); for example, in the loose employment of the term 'Puritan', whose imprecision I recognise but do not stop to take account of. The next chapter will try to demonstrate the validity, at least where Cowley is concerned, of my relative disregard of political and social contexts. Its subject is *The Civil War*, a poem which directly incorporates the raw material of history understood as the march of events, and a skeleton in Cowley's cupboard which the 1656 Preface mentions only in order to disavow.

2 Civil War

'I have cast away', Cowley declared in the Preface to the 1656 *Poems*, 'all such pieces as I wrote during the time of the late troubles, with any relation to the differences that caused them; as among others, *three Books of the Civil War it self*, reaching as far as the first *Battel* of *Newbury*, where the succeeding *misfortunes* of the *party* stopt the *work*' (P, 9). History, it seems, was to provide not only the subject-matter but also the plot of this poem; the poet was to follow as closely as possible in the wake of events, recorder rather than maker. But after the first Battle of Newbury history started to provide the wrong plot, and the poem failed. Despite Cowley's claim to have cast it away, a version of Book I was published in 1679 with the title *A Poem on the Late Civil War*, and two manuscript copies of the three completed books have recently been discovered by Allan Pritchard and made the basis of a proper edition of the poem. As the introduction and notes to that edition show, *The Civil War* did stick pretty close to history seen from a Royalist point of view; here surely is a case for a historicist reading, a poem whose 'form' and 'content' were both supposedly determined by history. But it seems to me that the poem had begun to fail, had moved into conflict with itself, *before* history started to provide the wrong plot. If we want to understand why it failed, we must examine not only its relation to history but also its spawning of relatively autonomous rhetorics which enter into conflict with themselves rather than with history.

The outbreak of civil war in 1642 forced Cowley to leave Cambridge, which was a militantly Puritan town, and he had probably arrived at the King's headquarters in Oxford by the end of the year. He started work on *The Civil War* during the summer or early autumn of 1643, and abandoned it after the first Battle of Newbury (20 September 1643). The poem opens with a discussion of the implications, rather than the actuality, of civil war:

7

> What rage does *England* from it selfe divide
> More then Seas doe from all the world beside?[1]

Civil war involves, above all, a redrawing of boundaries: the boundary which ought to be, and always used to be, drawn around England, unifying the nation against its enemies, has been redrawn so that it now divides the nation from itself. 'It was not soe', Cowley reiterates, during the reigns of Henry II, Richard Coeur de Lion, Edward III, Henry V and Elizabeth (lines 13–78). Thus, under Edward III, victory at the naval battle of Sluys initiated a series of victories including Crécy and Poitiers, and the sea itself constituted, as it were, the leading edge of national self-assertion:

> The'affrighted *Ocean* his first Conquest bore,
> And drove red waves to the sad *Gallick* shore.   (I, 41–2)

But civil war turned the edge of that force inwards, driving 'red waves' against and through the unity of the nation; already, with the first Bishops' War against the Scots, the boundary distinguishing friend from enemy had had to be redrawn inside rather than around the land-mass. For at the outset of that war the two armies found themselves encamped within sight of each other on either side of the Tweed:

> Just *Tweed*, that now had with long rest forgot
> On which side dwelt the *English*, which the *Scot*,
> Saw glittering Armes shine sadly on his face,
> Whilst all th'affrighted fish sunke downe apace.
>   (I, 97–100)

Events are now concentrated around the divisive river, a reactivated boundary, and although conflict was on this occasion avoided, the redrawing of the boundary within the land—and within minds—proved irreversible. Cowley's own attitude at this point seems to be one of disquiet rather than militancy, of bewilderment at a factionalism which has cut away the middle ground leaving only hostile extremes:

> To what with Worship the fond *Papist* falls,
> That the fond *Zealot* a curst *Idoll* calls.

So twixt their double madnes heres the odds,
One makes false *Devills*, t'other makes false *Gods*.   (I, 33–6)

The papist worships symbols, but the zealot overreacts by brand-
ing them as the works of the devil; both are foolishly credulous,
'fond', and the effect of their intransigence is to leave no place for
reason in matters of religion. The moderate in religion and in politics is now faced by the 'double madnes' of alternatives he can
neither avoid nor adopt. But in the political conflict Cowley
thought one party to be decisively at fault. The Grand Remon-
strance, which accused Charles of a whole series of offences, and
which was passed by the House of Commons on 22 November
1641, seemed to him utterly wilful:

> Through all the *excrements* of state they pry,
> Like *Emprickes* to find out a *Malady*.
> And then with desperate Boldnesse they endeavour,
> Th'*Ague* to cure by bringing in a *Feaver*:
> This way is sure to'expell some ills; noe doubt;
> The *Plague* will drive all lesse *Diseases* out:
> What strang wild Feares did every morning breed?
> Till a strang *fancy* made us sicke indeed·
> And *Cowardize* did *Valours* part supply,
> Like those that *kill* themselves for feare to *die*.
> What frantick diligence in these men appeares,
> That feare all ills, and act or'e all their *feares*?
> Thus into War we scar'ed our selves, and who
> But *Arons* Sonnes that the first *Trumpet* blew!
> Fond men! who knew not that they were to *keepe*
> For *God*, and not to *sacrifice* their *Sheepe*.
> The *Churches* first this murd'erous doctrine sow,
> And learne to *kill* as well as *bury* now.   (I, 111–28)

Cowley wants to define civil war as a psychological aberration:
'Thus into War we scar'ed our selves'. Wit discovers secret incongruities beneath apparently assured behaviour and in times of
civil war, when assurance freezes into defiance, the incongruities
multiply, churches 'learne to *kill* as well as *bury* now'. Wit, the
register of abnormality, becomes under such circumstances the
only 'normality', the only possible adaptive measure for anyone

like Cowley himself who can neither escape from the conflict nor take sides in it.

But the situation can no longer be controlled by those who initiated it:

> They call for *blood* which now I feare do's call,
> For *bloud* againe much louder then them all.   (I, 141–2)

Bloodshed perpetuates itself; 'sencelesse Clamours and confused Noyse' (I, 143) drown even the possibility of clarity and harmony. By securing the navy, on 2 July 1642, Parliament seems to have appropriated the very 'frame' of national purpose and identity:

> The *Sea* they subject next to their Commands,
> The *Sea* that Crownes our *Kings*, and all their *Lands*.
>
> (I, 165–6)

By usurping a domain emblematic of national unity, Parliament has condemned the country to divisive conflict, a conflict now carried forward by a succession of land-battles. The first major engagement of the war was the Battle of Edgehill, on 22 October 1642:

> On two faire *Hills* both Armies next are seene,
> Th'affrighted *Valley* sighes and sweates betweene.
>
> (I, 207–8)

In fact, while Charles's army did occupy the height of Edgehill, that commanded by the Earl of Essex was drawn up on a plain to the east, and not on any corresponding hill. But Cowley was primarily concerned to mark the boundary between two equal and opposing forces, a boundary reproduced in the text by means of a specific rhetorical device:

> Here *Angells* did with faire expectance stay
> And wisht good thinges to a *King* as mild as *they*.
> There *Fiends* with hungry waiting did abide;
> And curst both but spur'd on the guilty side.
> Here stood *Religion*, her lookes gently sage;
> *Aged*, but much more comely for her *age*.
> There *Schisme*, old *Hag*, but seeming young appeares,

As *snakes* by casting skin renew their yeares.
Undecent rages of severall dies she wore
And in her hands torne *Liturgies* she bore.
Here *Loyalty* an humble *Crosse* displaid
And still as *Charles* past by she bowd and prayd.
Sedition there her crimson *Banner* spreads,
Shakes all her Hands, and roares with all her Heads.
Her knotty haires were with dire *Serpents* twist,
And all her *Serpents* at each other hist.   (I, 209–24)

The geographic line of division has become an act of discrimination ('Here . . . There . . .'), separating 'us' from 'them', saved from damned, pure from impure. The responsibility for division can then be projected onto the 'other side'; sedition is not only plural, but also split from itself ('And all her *Serpents* at each other hist'). Cowley's rhetoric has now taken sides for him, even rationalising the difference between the Royalist and Parliamentarian dead at Edgehill as a difference of *kind*:

Streames of blacke tainted blood the field besmeare,
But pure wel-colour'd Drops shine here and there.
They scorne to mixe with floods of baser veines,
Just as th'ignobler Moistures *Oyle* disdaines.   (I, 277–80)

Again, one feels that Cowley's venomous rhetoric—note the placing of 'besmeare' and 'disdaines' at the end of the line—has taken up a position beyond his earlier, relatively undecided sense of bewilderment. Even the land now has its bias. The river Tamar, for example, the boundary between Cornwall and Devon, separated, during the winter of 1642–3, the territory held by the King from that held by Parliament:

Hee kist the *Cornish* Banks and vow'd to bring,
His richest waves to feed th'ensuing Spring,
But murmur'd sadly and almost denide,
All fruitfull Moisture to the *Devon* side.   (I, 411–4)

Whereas the Tweed had remained neutral, a mirror to war (like Cowley himself at that point), the Tamar actively discriminates.

Cowley's rhetoric has taken him deeper into civil conflict, swung him closer to one pole of the 'double madnes', than perhaps he had intended. It proves impossible to say anything without taking sides and once the boundary has been drawn between 'us' and 'them' everyone on the other side of it can be regarded, by definition, as corrupt or perverse. But to take sides in this way is to fight on the same terms as the enemy, to forfeit any claim to a transcendent point of view. Cowley therefore needs to persuade himself and his reader that Royalist does not in fact exist on the same level as Republican; that the chaos of civil war is part of a dialectical scheme and will be assimilated to a higher, more stable order, a hope vested largely in the person and quasi-divine function of the King:

> In his great lookes what cheerfull anger shone!
> Sad *warre* and joyfull *Triumph* mixt in one!   (I, 255–6)

The King is the locus of reconciliation, the place where contraries which would tear an ordinary man apart are resolved into a higher unity; his actions have a different frame of reference altogether. Thus, when Charles raised his standard at Nottingham on 22 August 1642, Cowley tells us, an army gathered with almost miraculous speed:

> When straight whole *Armies* meete in *Charles* his right,
> How noe man knowes; but here they are, and fight:
> A Man would sweare that saw his alter'd state,
> *Kings* were call'd *Gods* because they could *create*.
> Vaine men! tis heaven this swift assistance bringes;
> The same is *Lord* of *Hosts*, thats *King* of *Kings*.
> Had men forsooke him, *Angells* from above
> (The *Assyrian Host* did lesse their Justice move)
> Would all have muster'd in his righteous ayd,
> And *thunder* 'gainst your *Canon* would have playd.
> It needes not soe; for man desires to right
> Abusd *Mankind*; and, Wretches, yee must Fight.   (I, 169–80)

There can be no doubt about the immediate purpose of Cowley's remarks ('Wretches, yee must Fight'), but he was primarily concerned to show that the Royalist cause had a divine sanction and could call upon powers which operated at a different level of efficiency from that of mere men. His wit, when applied to the Royalist rather than the Parliamentarian cause, could reveal the secret cause of apparently natural occurrences; the '*Lord* of *Hosts*' must by definition be a good recruiting officer. But the possibility of a restoration of order is also maintained by the dominant imagery of river and sea, and, in particular, by the supposed loyalty of the River Thames:

> Thou griev'st to see the *white-nam'd pallace* shine,
> Without the Beames of its owne *Lord* and *Thine*.
> Thy *Lord*, who is to all as good and free,
> As thow, Kind *Flood*, to thine owne Banks canst bee.
> How do'es thy peacefull backe disdaine to beare,
> The rebells busie Pride from *Westminster*?
> Thow who thy Selfe, dost without Murmur pay
> Aeternall *Tributes* to thy *Prince*, the Sea!   (I, 337–44)

The ordered circulation of river and sea, the one paying tribute to the other, is emblematic of the proper state of society—an equilibrium of elements disturbed by the 'rebells busie Pride'. The image derives, as Pritchard notes, from Denham's *Coopers Hill*,[2] which was first published at London in August 1642, and reprinted at Oxford in April 1643. Cowley was thus contributing to an established symbolism, as he was when he described the meeting of Charles and Henrietta Maria at Kineton on 13 July 1643 in terms of a masque:

> Through the glad vale ten thousand *Cupids* fled,
> And chac'ed the wandring *Spirits* of *Rebells* dead.
> Still the lowd sent of *powder* did they feare,
> And scatterd *Easterne Smells* through all the Aire.
>   (I, 497–500)

The function of Stuart masque was to enact the dispelling of Chaos by Order, and elements from it could easily be adapted to Cowley's purpose here. The whole sense, throughout Book I, of a divine context to human fallibility and malevolence allows him a resolute concluding prayer:

> *Father of Peace*, mild *Lamb*, and gaullesse *Dove*,
> Gently allay, restore to us our sight,
> And then, oh, say once more, *Let there bee Light*.
> Speake to the restlesse *Sword*, and bid it stay,

> Stop *Plague* and *Famine* whilst they're yet o'th'way.
> But if that still their stubborne *Hearts* they fence,
> With new *Earth-workes* and shut thee out from thence,
> Goe on, great *God*, and fight as thou has fought.
> Teach them, or let the *world* by them be taught.   (I, 568–76)

Book I describes the genesis of civil war, the splitting of a nation from itself, but it still adheres to a transcendent frame of reference which may ultimately contain and heal the divisions. For the '*Earth-workes*' with which the rebels fence 'their stubborne *Hearts*' are not only military fortifications but also ramparts of human corruption erected against divine illumination.

In Book II, which gives a more extended account of the nature of this corruption, the imagery of earth and underground den predominates. Birmingham, captured by Prince Rupert on 3 April 1643, had supplied Essex's army with weapons, and so Cowley compares its inhabitants to the Cyclops Pyracmon and Brontes, assistants of Vulcan, who worked in the forge under Aetna:

> Downe falls the barbarous *Cyclops* sooty race.
> They knock the Earth, and every cave around
> *Ecchoes* as lowd, as to their *Anviles* sound.   (II, 78–80)

During the same month, Rupert recaptured the fortified cathedral close of Lichfield by mining the walls:

> The labouring Spade and Pick-axe sound below.
> With a dire noyse the earth and wall is rent,
> High into aire th'unwilling Stones are sent.
> Twice all about, the ground did tremble there,
> First with the violent *shock*, and nexte with *Feare*.
> The wicked *Guards* thought t'had some *Earthquake* binne,
> Their Soules confest the guilt of Korahs Sinne.   (II, 116–22)

Korah rebelled against Moses and was destroyed, with his followers, by an earthquake: 'And the earth opened her mouth, and swallowed them up, and their houses, and all the men that appertained unto Korah, and all their goods' (Numbers 16, 32). The imagery of cave and earthquake is further supplemented by that of an underground den. After Essex's abandonment of his advance on Oxford, and Waller's defeat at Roundway Down, the two generals retreated to London:

> Both to their *Dens*, well worried both, retreat,
> There snarle, and grinne, and brag which *lest* was beat.
>
> (II, 199–200)

This whole scheme of imagery, always associated with Republican rather than Royalist troops, prepares the way for Cowley's account of hell (365 ff.), the source of all sedition. Hell is situated 'deepe below' the 'silent Chambers of the Earth', below 'the dens, where unflecht Tempests ly' and 'the mighty Oceans wealthy caves'. It is peopled by 'Rebel Minds' in 'envious torments', and all manner of biblical dissidents:

> Good God! what hoasts has this worst Feind of Death,
> Sent mangled to th'unlovely Lands beneath.
> There factious Korah and his murm'urers roare;
> Still curse great Moses, but themselves much more.
> Through gapeing gulfs thether alive they fell;
> And skipt o're the first Death, with hast to Hell.   (II, 421–6)

Cowley obviously intended to implicate his political opponents in a larger, cosmic design of rebellion and corruption, and to ensnare them in an equally extensive web of imagery; like Milton's Satan, they are condemned to vertigo. The symbolism of earthquake and sapping, of 'gapeing gulfs' in the earth's surface, was particularly appropriate to the literal and spiritual consequences of civil war. Similarly, the 'dreadfull Parlament' summoned by Satan—

> Deepe in a dismall den, Bel-zebubs Hall,
> The Feinds all meet at their grimme Soveraignes call
>
> (II, 507–8)

—attaches sinister connotations to the proceedings of the Parliamentary opposition. Having thus inserted the events of the Civil War into a cosmic frame of reference, a dialectic larger than that of skirmish, Cowley could put his faith in the development of this scheme towards the defeat of Satan by Christ. For the poem is also, as Pritchard points out, moulded by epic tradition: 'Cowley appears to have in mind a common epic pattern, found for example in Tasso and later followed by Milton. In this pattern the forces of good secure an initial success; there is then an upsurge of the forces of evil, but in the conclusion good achieves an over-whelming triumph.'[3] Epic structure, even more than the symbolic role allocated to Charles, was to guarantee the validity of a tran-scendent frame of reference, a dialectic which would incorporate and transform the chaos described by Book II. As Charles had been able to reconcile destructive contraries, so the embracing epic structure would subsume and objectify Cowley's partisan rhetoric.

Unfortunately, however, neither monarch nor genre proved that resilient. Long before history ensured its redundancy the epic frame had been sapped from within by the play of antagonistic rhetorics. At the beginning of Book III Cowley describes the emergence of the Furies from hell to corrupt and incite the citizens of London:

> The Will they poyson, and the Reason wound,
> Leave the pale Conscience blinded, gagd, and bound,
> All ornaments of Nature, Art, or Grace
> (Like Zealots in faire Churches) they deface.   (III, 13–16)

Here, the frame of reference is provided by the abstract elements of the cosmic scheme—Will, Reason, Nature, Art, Grace—while actual events are relegated to an amplifying parenthesis. But the remaining narrative in effect reverses this relationship, bracketing off the cosmic scheme, and at the same time the unifying epic structure breaks down into a variety of styles. The first of these styles, describing the inflammatory activities of the Furies, is satiric:

> A thowsand arts and thowsand slights they frame
> T'avert the dangers of sweet Peaces name.
> To Westminster they hast, and fondly there,
> Talke, plot, conspire, vote, cov'enant, and declare.
> New feares, new hopes, pretences new they show,
> Whilst ore the wondring Towne their nets they throw.
> Up rose their Priests (the viperous brood that dare
> With their owne mouths their beawteous Mother tare).
> Their walking noysy diligence nere will cease;
> They roare, and sigh, and pray, and eate 'gainst peace.
>   (III, 31–40)

Cowley's target is again the perversity of the Puritan ministers who attack their own 'beawteous Mother', the Church. The series of nouns or verbs was to become a staple device of seventeenth-century satire, prominent for example in John Oldham's *Satires upon the Jesuits*; it satirised the frantic multiplicity of motive found in the social group under attack, a confusion ordered and superseded by the ascetic efficiency of the couplet. But even the couplet can barely control the catalogue of heretics:

> The rest who sent in lesser helpes to theise,
> Was Marcion, Nestorius, Eutiches,
> Montanus, Marcus, and Sabellius,
> Donatus, frantick Manes, Audius,
> Besides th'Apostolicks, and Encratites,
> Angelicalls, Jovinians, Hieracites.
> Paulists, Priscillians, Origenians,
> Cerinthians, and Nicolaitans. (III, 171–8)

And so on. The singularity of the verb introducing this list is nicely judged, suggesting that the various heresies constitute a single crime, and are all the more perverse for that. But the rhymes which bind this confusion into an ordering structure hardly register, for the trace of compatibility on sectarian and heretic will be faint indeed. However accurate these attacks may be, their rampant urgency introduces into the epic plan a potentially disruptive element, a rhetoric whose incorporation alters the nature of the poem.

This disruption intensifies during the account of the Battle of Newbury (20 September 1643) which takes up most of the Book. Before the battle, Charles and Essex address their respective armies, Charles resolutely ('Truth was in all hee said'), Essex 'with powrelesse words'. Cowley again draws the rhetorical boundary, as Charles points out to his men the 'diff'erence twixt your foes and yow':

> Yow all one Church binds close, I'me sure the most;
> More Sects then Squadrons fill their spotted Host.
> Your births command yow to orecome or dy;
> They their Forefathers wrong unlesse they fly. (III, 295–8)

But this time the rhetorical discrimination develops rapidly into an opposition of styles. At Edgehill, the distinctions between the two armies ('Here . . . There . . .'), and between the Royalist and Parliamentarian dead, had been descriptive, made from the point of view of an omniscient narrator. At Newbury, Cowley adopts one style, satire, for the Parliamentarian dead (lines 383–454), and another, elegy, for the Royalist dead (lines 455–648). There are now two realities, each constituted by a different literary mode, which cannot be included within a single epic or narrative decorum. The boundary between 'us' and 'them' has been drawn so firmly that the two parties inhabit contradictory realities, and the division which is the poem's subject has finally entered into its very structure. Cowley still tries to apply the transcendent frame of reference to Cavalier saint and Roundhead devil, but one can have no confidence that the scheme will be carried through to its proper conclusion, since the epic structure has been superseded by an irresolvable antagonism between modes. There is no longer any overall system of established values and procedures into which people and events might be fitted, and the poet has therefore to make sense out of experience without reference to any such overall system. Epic decorum makes no provision for Parliamentarian heroes:

> What should I here their Great ones Names reherse?
> Low, wretched Names, unfit for noble Verse?   (III, 383–4)

So Cowley has to find for them a satiric language, a code of remembrance appropriate to their criminality. Not even the most heroic language, on the other hand, can do justice to the Royalist dead:

> And would my Verse were nobler for your sake!
> (III, 462)

Cowley's lament for them has a kind of pessimistic intensity, as if no ultimate victory could compensate for the loss. The problem is that, however appropriate these different styles may seem to their subjects, any work which employs them both at the same time will be deeply fissured, at cross purposes with itself. In *The Civil War*, neither of the two styles can perform the encompassing function of epic structure, since they only exist in relation to each other, equal and opposite. Furthermore, each one represents not so much an established decorum, as a gesture towards meaning, an attempt to make sense out of inexplicable occurrences. This is particularly true of the account of Falkland's death, where Cowley makes no attempt to fit his own subjective response into a generalised decorum:

> An aesterne wind from Newb'ury rushing came,
> It sigh'd, meethoughts, it sigh'd out Falklands Name.
> Falkland, meethoughts, the Hills all Eccho'ed round,
> Falkland, meethoughts, each Bird did sadly sound.
> A Muse stood by mee, and just then I writ
> My Kings great acts in Verses not unfit.
> The trowbled Muse fell shapelesse into aire,
> Instead of Inck dropt from my Pen a Teare.
> O 'tis a deadly Truth! Falkland is slaine;
> His noble blood all dyes th'accursed plaine.   (III, 541–50)

As Pritchard points out, an earlier version of the conceit in lines 547–8 had appeared in Cleveland's contribution to *Justa Edouardo King*; it belonged, in other words, to elegy rather than to epic. Dryden thought that Cowley's fondness for this type of witty turn, which he considered unsuitable for heroic verse, had ruined the *Davideis*. Cowley's attempt to come to terms with Falkland's death must be related, not to epic models, but to one of his earlier occasional poems, 'To the Lord Falkland. For his safe Return from the Northern Expedition against the Scots'. He addressed Falkland, conventionally enough, as a '*Prince* of *Knowledge*' and as a paradigm of *discordia concors*, claiming that the contents of wisdom

> In his unbounded Breast *engraven* are.
> There all the *Sciences* together meet,
> And every *Art* does all her *Kindred* greet,
> Yet justle not, nor quarrel; but as well
> Agree as in some *Common Principle*.   (P, 19)

Yet this praise in terms of an established system of values is not adequate to the situation, because the '*Prince* of *Knowledge*' has been thrust 'into th'noise and business of a State', called away to war:

> Whilst we who can no action undertake,
> Whom *Idleness* it self might *Learned* make,
> Who hear of nothing, and as yet scarce know,
> Whether the *Scots* in *England* be or no,
> Pace dully on, oft tire, and often stay,
> Yet see his nimble *Pegasus* fly away.

The verse catches the note of anxious boredom ('Pace dully on, oft tire, and often stay'), introducing into the poem a purely subjective element—the scansion of mood rather than of a public value-system. There is now the further question of how an individual responds to the type of social paradigm represented by Falkland, particularly when that paradigm has been placed under threat of destruction. Cowley's only answer is that the paradigm ought to be preserved from the flux of experience:

> He is too good for *War*, and ought to be
> As far from *Danger*, as from *Fear* he's free.

The lament for Falkland in *The Civil War* can be seen as a grim recognition of the naïveté of this view; the paradigm has encountered danger, and been destroyed. As a result, the apprehensiveness of 'To the Lord Falkland' has turned into the bewilderment of a man at the limit of his resources:

> I see, I see each Virtue and each Art,
> Crowd through the gapeing Wound from out his Heart.
> In a long row through the glad aire they runne,
> Like Swarmes of guilded Atomes from the Sunne.
>
> (III, 571–4)

It is as if Cowley were unravelling the images of *discordia concors* which had made up his earlier poem, recognising that the locus of their integration has removed elsewhere. He does grant Falkland a triumphant apotheosis, but one is left with a sense of irreversible pessimism, rather than the conviction of a painful but necessary sacrifice on the way to the eventual overthrow of evil:

> Wretches, your losse will now triumphant bee,
> You'le Falkland name when wee name Victorie.
>
> (III, 623–4)

The relation of an individual to the paradigms provided by his society—more strictly, his relation to the means he has of representing those paradigms to himself—has become problematic. It is not so much civil war as the conflict between the attitudes it is possible to take to civil war which invalidates epic structure. Caught in a fierce oscillation between satire and elegy, a language for 'them' and a language for 'us', Cowley found the epic frame increasingly inhospitable. He abandoned the poem when the course of events turned against the King, but it was already a deeply flawed undertaking, its rhetorics even more intractable than its subject-matter. Looking for a triumphant form and a triumphant style, it discovered only its own divisiveness.

3 The Lyrics

I

'*Poets*', Cowley declared in the Preface to the 1656 *Poems*, 'are scarce thought *Free-men* of their *Company*, without paying some duties, and obliging themselves to be true to *Love*. Sooner or later they must all pass through that *Tryal*' (P, 10). The 'trial' is regulated by already established conventions, which the initiate cannot ignore, although he may try to modify them; it will entail the observance of conventions, rather than self-expression. One should not, Cowley argued, judge the 'manners' of a lyric poet from his 'writings', because poetry is 'not the *Picture* of the *Poet*, but of *things* and *persons* imagined by him' (P, 10). This picture was to be composed in accordance with or opposition to conventions and procedures which it will be the purpose of the present chapter to examine.

Were the rules governing the 'trial' Cowley had undertaken common to the love-poetry of all ages, or specific to Renaissance lyric? *The Mistress* draws equally on Ovid (especially the *Ars Amatoria*) and on modern lyricists: Spenser, Donne, Suckling, Waller. But it seems to me that its procedures can best be understood in relation to Renaissance models, and indeed it was an axiom of neoclassical criticism that classical love-poetry and modern love-poetry constituted separate discourses. Classical love-poetry, according to William Walsh, was relevant to the experience of most men, whereas the Moderns have 'sought out for Occasions, that none meet with, but themselves; and fill their Verses with thoughts that are surprizing and glittering, but not tender, passionate, or natural to a Man in Love'. Dryden felt that Cowley's love-poetry, like Donne's, was forbiddingly intellectual and John Oldmixon, discussing 'A Valediction: Forbidding Mourning', pursued the same line of argument:

What Woman's Heart in the World could stand out against such an Attack as this, after she once understood how to handle a Pair of Compasses? Both *Donne* and *Cowley* were Men of Learning, and must consequently have read the Antients over and over. They could never learn this from them, but owe all their Extravagance in it to their own Genius's.[1]

The Moderns have chosen the same subject-matter as the Ancients, but they handle it in an entirely different way; they emphasise their own ingenuity at the expense of common experience, they surprise without convincing (essentially Johnson's criticism of 'Metaphysical' verse). This distinction between classical and modern would be accepted, although as a commendation rather than a criticism, by H. M. Richmond, whose book *The School of Love* represents the most thorough and consistent attempt yet to provide a context for the Stuart lyric. He argues for a continuous 'evolution of sensibility' from classical to Stuart love-poetry, the latter achieving a greater level of intellectual sophistication and of technical competence than any of its predecessors. Thus, for Renaissance lyricists alert to the implications of 'analytical psychology', love was not simply the 'physical satisfaction of sensual desire', as it had been for classical poets, but rather a 'tension of mental attitudes'. The greater capacity, even among minor poets, for 'succinct and forceful lyrical expression' meant that there was a 'margin of energy' left for 'further creative impulse beyond the search for a firm statement of sentiment that is characteristic of much classical lyricism'.[2] While remaining sceptical about Richmond's evolutionism, I think that his main point about the distinctness of classical and modern love-poetries stands, and that his account of the characteristics of Stuart lyric shows Cowley to have been initiating himself into a specifically modern discourse.

But why was the love-lyric a form so compelling and so prestigious that Cowley felt obliged to try his hand at it, regardless of whether or not he had had any experience in *ars amatoria*? Try his hand, that is, eighty-four times. Could it be that this private and retrusive form had become 'privileged'? I mean that the positions provided by the lyric (lover, loved, rival) and the relations established between them (dominance, subordination, envy)—apparently so specific—had acquired an unusual generality of application. In the first instance, since the 'lover' is usually male and the 'loved' female (which would certainly not be true of classical love-poetry), any lyric is always already a comment on the particular stereotyping of sexual and gender roles in contemporary society. So much is obvious. But beyond that the form was 'ripe' for appropriation, charged with non-specific relevance, in a way the verse-epistle, say, or the elegy were not. Queen Elizabeth, indeed, was able to appropriate the conventions of lyric discourse for political ends, by placing herself in the position of mistress as defined by Petrarchan protocol and her courtiers in the position of supplicant lover, and by living the relation of power thus produced. Furthermore, lover and mistress are usually related as subject to object (he perceives and speaks, she is perceived and spoken about), so that any lyric could be a comment on what it 'means' to be subjectified or objectified; this is certainly true of many poems in *The Mistress*. The relation between lover and mistress is, however, by no means immutable; for it is not given to us, but rather produced by a certain coding. A tone of plaint, for example, codes the lover as inferior to his mistress, while a tone of outrageous hyperbole codes him as superior; different codes produce different relations of power. It would clearly have been impolitic for Elizabeth to place herself in the mistress-position defined by Donne's 'The Flea', had she been able to.

II

It is because these codes change that we do not read a love-lyric by Donne in the same way as we read a love-lyric by Samuel Daniel. Sonnet 9 of *Delia* and 'The Flea' both position lover and mistress; both communicate about their own communications, guiding us to an interpretation; but these (meta)communications differ, each one producing a different relation between lover and mistress, a different kind of 'message'. The sonnet-cycles of the 1590s placed the mistress in a position of dominance by defining her as the locus of paradox, as sonnet 60 of *Astrophil and Stella* demonstrates:

> WHEN my good Angell guides me to the place,
>   Where all my good I do in *Stella* see,
>   That heav'n of joyes throwes onely downe on me
>   Thundred disdaines and lightnings of disgrace:
>   But when the ruggedst step of Fortune's race

Makes me fall from her sight, then sweetly she
With words, wherein the Muses' treasure be,
Shewes love and pitie to my absent case.
Now I, wit-beaten long by hardest Fate,
So dull am, that I cannot looke into
The ground of this fierce *Love* and lovely hate:
Then some good body tell me how I do,
Whose presence, absence, absence presence is;
Blist in my curse, and cursed in my blisse.

The wit-beaten lover cannot decide which of his mistress's contradictory actions are meant; she always does what he least expects.
He cannot make sense of her 'fierce *Love* and lovely hate', and the
result of this bewilderment is the immobility defined by the syn-
tactic suspension of the penultimate line; an immobility ruptured,
in Sidney's case, by the promptings of appetite, but characteristic
of the kind of Petrarchan lover described by Henry Constable:

Loe; in suspence of feare, and hope, upholden,
diversly poyz'd, with passions that paine mee,
no resolution dares my thoughts imbolden,
since tis not I, but thou that doost sustaine mee.

The lover, diversely poised among contradictory passions, irres-
olute, would seem to be entirely in the power of his mistress. How
does he cope with this humiliating loss of identity? By claiming
that the behaviour of his mistress was inevitable, that the event described had no significance because it simply repeated an original
Event, an original and as yet unexpiated rejection. According to
Constable the lover is 'no modell figure, or signe of care', but
rather the essence of care itself, 'in whom griefes comentaries written are'. Grief's commentaries constitute the code which enables
us to interpret the meaning of a particular message, the plight of
an individual lover. The lover himself is both message—the subject of a particular experience, an act of speech—and code—the
sum of inherited wisdom, the immutable language of grief. He is
both a message interpreted according to a certain code, and a
message which itself maintains and reinvents that code, and so is
absolved of individual responsibility; a distinction wittily ex-
ploited by Sidney:

STELLA oft sees the verie face of wo
   Painted in my beclowded stormie face:
   But cannot skill to pitie my disgrace,
Not though thereof the cause her selfe she know:
Yet hearing late a fable, which did show
   Of Lovers never knowne, a grievous case,
   Pitie thereof gate in her breast such place
That, from that sea deriv'd, teares' spring did flow.
   Alas, if Fancy drawne by imag'd things,
Though false, yet with free scope more grace doth breed
Then servant's wracke, where new doubts honor brings;
Then thinke my deare, that you in me do reed
   Of Lover's ruine some sad Tragedie:
   I am not I, pitie the tale of me.[3]

Sidney argues that Stella should regard him not as himself (an un-
fortunate individual), but rather as a reincarnation of the experience of grief; not as message but as code. Since she has proved so
susceptible to the code, she ought to recognise that the code (the
fable) has been rewritten in him: 'I am not I, pitie the tale of me'.

   The Petrarchan lover understands himself not as an individual
but as a ritual sacrifice to paradox; Cupid's arrows have found
their 'mark', he is both *target*—the man singled out for this fate—
and *record*—a ritual object scored by the 'burning markes' of his
mistress's look. This record demonstrates the validity of his commitment, by describing the worth of his mistress and also the suffering which that commitment has caused: 'Her praise from my
complaint I may not part' (Daniel). Praise involves a reading of
'the faire text' of the mistress's person, a noting of 'each character
of blisse' written there (Sidney). These signs constitute the field of
the poet's attention, a 'stay to fancy-traces' (Greville), and they
also determine the form of his complaint:

     O then I love, and drawe this weary breath,
     For her the cruell faire, within whose brow
     I written finde the sentence of my death,
     In unkinde letters; wrought she cares not how.[4]

The 'weary breath' of the sonneteer, his individual act of expression, reinvents and maintains the language of paradox, of
cruel fairness. Each poem becomes a ritual object, a mnemonic

icon on which the history of love is inscribed and its latest incarnation celebrated: 'I . . . seeke in verse to carve thee out' (Constable). As with any form of ritual, many enactments may be required in order to make sense of a particular experience, in order to assimilate an event to the original, founding Event. So the sonneteer, caught in the 'circle of my sorrowes never ending' (Daniel), must go on repeating himself: 'Say all, and all well sayd, still say the same' (Sidney). Saying the same means saying it in the same way each time, and the even constancy of form and tone in many Elizabethan sonnet-sequences has been remarked on often enough. The burning marks of his mistress's scorn engrave a kind of tribal memory on the body of the lover, who thus becomes assimilated to collective experience and survives a rejection which would otherwise have been hard to take. His ritualised commentaries on grief are themselves furthermore complicit with locutionary truth, since in each case we attend to 'the person propounding' rather than to 'the proposition itself'; we receive a message whose function is to sustain a familiar frame of reference, not to assert its own uniqueness. That frame of reference may not always, or indeed often, produce good poems, but it nearly always produces intelligible poems.

Even the work of ironists like Sidney and Greville presupposed familiarity with an existing frame of reference, and could be understood by its testing of or deviance from a norm. But other poets, notably Donne, did begin to challenge the established conventions from the outside rather than from the inside. The nature and extent of that challenge has, of course, long been a matter of debate, but to avoid recapitulating the debate I shall rest my case on evidence drawn from an essay by the minor poet and critic Dudley North, written around 1610–12. North assumed that lyric verse should be governed by conveniency, by the exact and equal fit of each element to an immanent pattern; stanza-form was not something to be adapted to the inflexions of the speaking voice, but primary, given in advance, a symmetrical mould. Diffused over such a pattern, brought at each point to an equivalent sheen, language itself testified to the justness of measured limit. North remarked unfavourably on the emergence of a new and innovatory poetic which, among other things, was disrupting the pattern proper to lyric verse by its barbarous preoccupation with such devices as enjambement. It cannot, he argued, 'bee good in limited lines, which are a purposed pause to the voyce, to carry

with a counter-time the period of the sense to the body of the next
line, much lesse to dismember an innocent word'.[5] Perhaps he was
remembering the bravado with which Donne, in Satire IV, had
split words like 'forget-full' and 'egge-shels' over line-endings. At
any rate, his objection to enjambement was that it introduced a
'counter-time', a rhythm moving against or beneath the patterned
fitness of the verse-form. Furthermore, this interest in coun-
ter-times seemed characteristic of a general disregard for patterned fitness, in terms of imagery as well as of prosody:

> Conceits and matter over-crusht, afford commonly as little
> grace as pleasure; and to write all in abbreviations, would take
> indeed lesse room, but much more time and trouble. A *Geneva*
> print weakens the sight, nor is it good to hold your bow ever
> bent, or your horse streight reined. Sometimes amongst pithy
> and tough lines I thinke it not amisse to interpose one of an easie
> straine, like resting places in lofty staires, to ease the Reader.

North considered that verse should be 'delightfull and pleasant to
the first appearance with conveniency to the designe': spacious,
apparent, harmonious, decorous. The new emphasis on concen-
tration of form and matter was clearly at variance with such principles. But North's approach is important chiefly because it takes
account of the effect of technical innovations on the reader. For the
spaciousness of Elizabethan verse, its readiness to interpose lines
'of an easie straine, like resting places in lofty staires', told the
reader what kind of significance to expect from the poem. It provided the frame of reference according to which a poem could be
interpreted, the set of conventions which defined it as ritual. By
contrast, the code according to which a poem by Donne might be
interpreted, whatever currency it had among the circle of those
privileged to receive the manuscripts of such poems, was unknown
to North. He could not approve 'the ridling humour lately affected
by many, who thinke nothing good that is easie, nor any thing
becomming passion that is not exprest with an hyperbole above
reason'. This remark signals the emergence of a new code which
trades on its own excess, producing poems to be enjoyed for their
extravagance, their breaking of bounds, rather than for their conveniency. There had of course been among Donne's immediate
predecessors poets whose work revealed a sufficiently 'ridling
humour', a preoccupation with the refinements of wit: Sidney,

Greville, Chapman. But Donne establishes wit as the major frame of reference for his secular poetry. His more rakish lyrics, which had the greater influence on subsequent poets, advertise themselves as witty exercises. The emphatic casuistry and the 'hyperbole above reason' of these lyrics tell the reader exactly how they are to be read: as demonstrations of intelligence. The main point of such poems is, as Leishman puts it, 'that they should be felt to be outrageous—that, indeed, a very large measure of immediately perceptible outrageousness and exaggeration is of the very essence of their wit'; and Kermode remarks that 'we are aware that we are being cleverly teased, but many of the love-poems, like "The Extasie" or "The Flea", depend on our wonder outlasting our critical attitude to argument'.[6] We may have trouble following the intricacies of Donne's casuistry, but we need be in no doubt as to what kind of poem we are dealing with; their surplus of 'immediately perceptible outrageousness and exaggeration' codes them as *jeux d'esprit*.

With Donne, for the first time, tone—the inflection of a speaking voice—becomes the most important coding device. We no longer derive pleasure from the fulfilment of pattern, from the exact fit of semantic to metrical unit, but rather from the sense of a mind displayed at the moment when it commits itself to language, a mind which seems to invent its own patterns as it goes along. Yet, when, but, if, or: these are the terms which deploy and intersect Donne's lyrics. Tone is solitary, has broken away from the dance, renegued on conveniency; it produces 'hyperbole above reason', the relishing of a dangerous freedom, 'this absolute right of dominion over all thoughts, that dukes are bid to clean his shoes, and are yet honoured by it! . . . this lordliness of opulence!'.[7] Exaggeration is now the medium in which the speaker of the poem moves, always prone to 'unsweare' or 'overswear' anything he has said (Elegy XVI), outwitting his mistress in order to assert dominion over her. The new code, in other words, produces a new relation between subject and object within the poem.

This description of the two major codes operating in lyric verse between Sidney and Rochester has been both schematic and tentative; but it is, I think, roughly accurate. The initiation rite Cowley underwent was regulated by two frames of reference, the second of which came into play during the early years of the century and produced technical innovations and a new relation between subject and object. Richmond describes this shift in more orthodox terms when he remarks that in Stuart love-poetry 'the power and authority of the individual consciousness in the face of the most bizarre and challenging circumstances are consistently vindicated . . . Lament, the hallmark of lovers from earliest times, but more particularly since the era of the troubadours, becomes less and less characteristic of love poetry. Instead, we hear a new note of virile self-confidence . . .'[8] 'Lament' and the 'new note of virile self-confidence' are the codes which defined what Cowley was able to say.

III

The Mistress opens with a poem entitled 'The Request':

> I'have often wisht to love; what shall I do?
>   Me still the *cruel Boy* does *spare*;
>   And I a double task must bear,
> First to woo *him*, and then a *Mistress* too.   (P, 65)

The 'double task' Cowley has set himself is to invent both code and message, both a set of conventions for the description of love (Cupid) and the specific wooings those conventions will produce. Donne had successfully performed such a double task, but only at the cost to lyric discourse of some instability. By the time Cowley wrote, instability had become endemic; one could either write poems which celebrated their own heroic marginality, as Marvell and the 'Cavalier' poets in various ways did, or one could massively and gloomily regret the inhospitality of familiar conventions, as Cowley did. There is no doubt in my mind as to which of these two possible courses of action produced the more enjoyable poetry, but *The Mistress* holds a kind of fascination for me because it registers from the inside the exhaustion of a discourse. Conventions whose functioning had seemed automatic suddenly fail, and their failure results in messages which seem as baffling to us as they did to the neo-classical critics who accused the impeccably sober and virginal Abraham Cowley of obscenity; a malign spectre haunts the whole machinery of Cupids and torrid zones and premature boasts. This process of the exhaustion of a form—in effect, of the two codes described in the preceding section—manifests itself either by a certain scepticism about (a wrily acknowledged failure to operate) established conventions, or by a 'becoming literal' of positions and statements which if adequately coded would leave a margin for irony. The second process—the failure of poems to communicate about their own communications—will be dealt with in the next section; here I want to discuss the ways in which certain poems in *The Mistress* 'come unstuck' when they attempt to reproduce familiar codes.

The poem which most obviously meditates the impossibility of coding is the neo-Spenserian epithalamium 'Her Name':

> With more than *Jewish Reverence* as yet
>   Do I the *Sacred Name* conceal;
> When, ye kind *Stars*, ah when will it be fit
>   This *Gentle Mystery* to reveal?
> When will our Love be *Nam'd*, and we possess
> That *Christning* as a *Badge* of *Happiness*?   (P, 135)

To name the lady would be to name their relationship, to code it in accordance with established convention, to give it a public identity like that bestowed on a child by the ritual of baptism. But until that happens she cannot even be worshipped in the customary manner, let alone possessed; so Cowley's epithalamium remains conditional, its celebratory rites stored up for the future:

> Then all the fields and woods shall with it ring;
>   Then *Ecchoes* burden it shall be;
> Then all the *Birds* in sev'eral notes shall sing,
>   And all the *Rivers* murmur Thee;
> Then ev'ery *wind* the Sound shall upwards bear,
> And softly whisper't to some *Angels* Ear.

This clearly echoes the refrain of Spenser's 'Epithalamion':

> Ah my deere love why doe ye sleepe thus long,
> When meeter were that ye should now awake,
> T'awayt the comming of your joyous make,
> And hearken to the birds lovelearned song,
> The dewy leaves among.
> For they of joy and pleasance to you sing,
> That all the woods them answer and theyr eccho ring.[9]

But, whereas Spenser's refrain ('That all the woods . . .') stands in a constantly changing relation to the events of the poem, as a kind of ritual frame, Cowley can only offer a celebratory tone isolated and immobilised by its precarious futurity. The poem, far from arriving at any triumphant conclusion, circles back to meditate its own deferment:

> Mean while I will not dare to *make a Name*
>   To represent thee by;
> *Adam (Gods Nomenclator)* could not frame
>   One that enough should *signifie*.
> *Astraea* or *Caelia* as unfit would prove
> For *Thee*, as 'tis to call the *Deity, Jove*.

During this deferment—produced, I would argue, by the failure of a code and lasting until the final word of *The Mistress* had been written—the lover will not presume to make a name for his mistress. Even the traditional code of Elizabethan lyricism—'*Astraea* or *Caelia* as unfit would prove'—has been exhausted. The poem flaunts its intimacy with conventions it cannot, finally, operate.

Another poem haunted by the redundancy of a traditional code is 'Her Unbelief', where the lover complains that his mistress has not even noticed the ritualised submissiveness he has laid out before her:

> That truly you my *Idol* might appear,
>   Whilst all the *People* smell and see
>   The odorous flames, I offer thee,
> Thou sit'st, and dost not see, nor smell, nor hear
>   Thy constant zealous *worshipper*.   (P, 141)

He has placed himself in the position of a worshipper at the shrine of paradox, and deploys the repertoire of gestures signifying that position, but without effect:

> *Fair Infidel!* by what unjust decree
>   Must I, who with such restless care
>   Would make this truth to thee appear,
> Must I, who preach it, and pray for it, be
>   Damn'd by thy *incredulitie*?

The episode seems to concern, on a small scale, a failure of locutionary truth, a failure on the part of 'the person propounding' to make his rhetoric register, let alone convince. The speaker wriggles out of despondency by a piece of rather uninteresting sophistry, but one is left feeling that this is a poem about the sudden failure of a convention which everyone had assumed would function automatically, if not always to good effect. I think that in 'Her Name' and in 'Her Unbelief' Cowley is pondering his own inability to write Elizabethan lyrics, lyrics which would unashamedly print out a collective memory instead of delivering the lover up to wry solitariness.

But he also felt, perhaps more strongly, the appeal of that alternative frame of reference implied by Donne's rakish lyrics, by 'The Will' or 'The Flea'. Again, though, the code fails him; the self-confidence, the 'immediately perceptible outrageousness and exaggeration', cannot be sustained. A comparison between Donne's 'Loves diet' and Cowley's 'My Dyet', both of which are concerned with the constraints it is possible to put on appetite, will make the point. 'Loves diet' announces itself immediately as a demonstration of intelligence:

> To what a combersome unwieldinesse
> And burdenous corpulence my love had growne,
> But that I did, to make it lesse,
> And keepe it in proportion,
> Give it a diet, made it feed upon
> That which love worst endures, *discretion*.[10]

The way in which the polysyllabic leviathans 'combersome unwieldinesse' and 'burdenous corpulence' are brought under control mimics the proposed subduing of appetite; form and theme coincide ostentatiously. Such immediately perceptible adroitness tells us to read the poem as a *jeu d'esprit*, to enjoy it without taking it literally:

> Thus I reclaim'd my buzard love, to flye
> At what, and when, and how, and where I chuse;
> Now negligent of sport I lye,
> And now as other Fawkners use,
> I spring a mistresse, sweare, write, sigh and weepe:
> And the game kill'd, or lost, goe talke, and sleepe.

The lordly indifference of the 'I' towards the verbs at its disposal marks the poem as an indulgence; the poet sports in the surplus of leisure over work, of insouciance over commitment, created by his verbal dexterity. And we, I think, know to relish his commanding felicity, without asking too many questions.

Cowley's 'My Dyet' does not imitate Donne's poem, but it may perhaps borrow from 'The Computation' and it certainly aims at a Donnean extravagance:

> Now *by my Love*, the greatest *Oath* that is,
>   None loves you half so well as I: ...   (P, 89)

This, surely, is 'hyperbole above reason'; but the remaining stanzas describe the *collapse* of that stridency, its failure to determine our reading of the poem. The opening lines, that is to say, lead us by their tone of deliberate overstatement to expect a Donnean exercise in out-witting; but the confidence visibly drains out of this bravado as the poem develops. In the first stanza the 'I' dominates, pleading, cajoling; in the last stanza units of measurement have asserted their supremacy over it, occupying the dominant position in each line and crowding it (by now object rather than subject) into helpless passivity:

> O'n a *Sigh* of Pity I a year can live,
>   One *Tear* will keep me twenty at least,
>   Fifty a gentle *Look* will give;
> An hundred years on one *kind word* I'll feast:
>   A thousand more will added be,
> If you an *Inclination* have for me;
> And all beyond is vast *Eternity*.

Whereas Donne had concluded 'Loves diet' by declaring—and demonstrating—complete control, Cowley can only admit powerlessness: 'And all beyond is vast *Eternity*'. When Marvell borrowed the pharse 'vast eternity' for 'To His Coy Mistress', he incorporated it into an elaborate structure of argument; in 'My Dyet' it simply registers the impossibility of argument.

This melancholy process—the collapse of stridency, the reversal of the 'I' from subject to object—structures many poems in *The Mistress*; it becomes an element of their *form*, a tonal slither which one learns to listen for. Sometimes it is handled quite subtly, as a way of ironising a preposterous assertion—for example, the Ovidian claim to be love's tutor ('praeceptor amoris') and love's prophet ('Me vatem celebrate, viri . . .'). In 'The Prophet' the speaker describes himself as the 'chief *Professour*' of love, but the poem puts this pose in question at the same time as proclaiming it:

'Tis I who *Love's Columbus* am; 'tis I,
  Who must new *Worlds* in it descry:
  Rich *Worlds*, that yield of *Treasure* more,
  Than all that has bin known before.
And yet like *his* (I fear) *my Fate* must be,
To find them out for *others*; not for *Me*.
  Me Times to come, I know it, shall
  Loves last and greatest *Prophet* call.
  But, ah, what's that, if she refuse,
To hear the wholesome *Doctrines* of my *Muse*?
If to my share the *Prophets fate* must come;
  Hereafter *Fame*, here *Martyrdome*.   (P, 102)

Prophecy has its disadvantages, and posthumous reputation is perhaps worth less than present satisfaction. This poem, in fact, shows that Cowley was perfectly capable of blending and ironising lyric traditions, for the relished incongruities of its first stanza imitate Donne's 'The Will', a lyric also quoted in the preface to the 1656 *Poems* (P, 8). Cowley undercuts both the arrogance of Ovid's pose and the rakish insouciance of Donne's manner; his poem recognises that self-assertiveness may intensify precisely at the moment when doubts are arising about its validity. Thus, in the stanza quoted, the interpolated 'I fear' counters the hubris of the preceding lines, finding unconsidered implications in the Columbus-image and initiating a movement of self-doubt. Stridency persists, in the talk of fame and martyrdom, but it has been challenged. In this case the assertiveness derives from Ovid and from Donne; more often, though, one feels that Cowley has internalised the tone of exaggeration, that he would like to believe it, but is ultimately forced to recognise its implausibility. Not only does Cowley have no actual mistress to woo, but he cannot even operate those conventions which signify the exuberant passion of a Donnean lover. The convention fails him and he again writes poems about his inability to write a certain kind of poem. His lyrics summon an excitable tone, protract it, then desist:

1

I know 'tis *sordid*, and 'tis *low*;
(All this as well as you I know)
Which I so hotly now pursue;
(I know all this as well as you)
But whilst this cursed flesh I bear,
And all the *Weakness*, and the *Baseness* there,
Alas, alas, it will be always so.

2

In vain, exceedingly in vain
I rage sometimes, and bite my *Chain*;
For to what purpose do I bite
With Teeth which ne're will break it quite?
For if the chiefest *Christian Head*,
Was by this sturdy *Tyrant buffeted*,
What wonder is it, if *weak I* be *slain*?   (P, 113)

The first stanza of this poem, 'The Frailty', emphasises above all the lover's fussy awareness ('I know') of his own desire, and the parentheses indicate that he is familiar with every aspect of 'all this'. Similarly, in 'The Prophet', Cowley had declared himself to be the 'chief *Professour*' of love and therefore not in need of instruction from anyone else. Desire may be morally reprehensible, but it undeniably proceeds from *self* and so constitutes a form of self-assertion; or so the first stanza of 'The Frailty' would have us believe. But who is this 'self' desire proceeds from and asserts? Is it the 'self' who says 'I know'? The second stanza of the poem would suggest not. The moment of self-assertion ('I rage') no longer dominates; it is preceded by a strong statement of helplessness ('In vain, exceedingly in vain'), qualified by 'sometimes', and defined by an image of enslavement ('bite my *Chain*'). Unanswerable questions supersede confident self-awareness, and desire is now seen as a '*Tyrant*' buffeting '*weak I*'. The introduction of the example of Solomon further removes the responsibility for desire so confidently assumed in the first stanza, as of course does the passive tense of the final verb. If the first stanza had imposed on moral weakness a cognitive strength—the unity of self-consciousness—then the second stanza demonstrates that such awareness is itself an illusion. The lover proves psychologically, as well as morally, frail, divided from himself by the tyranny of desire. Like the Cartesian *cogito*, Cowley's 'I know' rises out of and attempts to order the flux of experience, but only too easily collapses back into subjection. The lyrics of *The Mistress* play out the drama of the '*weak I*', using love as a metaphor for the field of experience. Desire invalidates the *cogito's* pretensions to stability and autonomy, a point made by 'The Encrease':

> I thought, I'll swear, I could have lov'd no more
> Then I had done before;
> But you as easi'ly might account
> 'Till to the *top* of *Numbers* you amount,
> As cast up my *Loves* score.
> Ten thousand millions was the sum;
> *Millions* of endless *Millions* are to come. (P, 122)

The flux of becoming destroys the claim of conscious thought to set a limit to and thus account for, experience. This flux is, furthermore, a result not of contingency but of self-division:

> A *real* cause at first did move;
> But mine own *Fancy* now drives on my Love,
> With *shadows* from it self that flow.

The shadows which drive on desire flow from, and also away from, '*Fancy*'; they invalidate any attempt to exert conscious control by distinguishing between real and unreal, or by the establishment of limits described in the opening lines. The lover is forced to admit that he has become the slave of his desires, object rather than subject, moved rather than mover:

> So the new-made, and untride *Spheres* above,
> Took their first turn from th'hand of *Jove*;
> But are since that beginning found
> By their own Forms to move for ever round.
> All *violent Motions* short do prove,
> But by the length 'tis plain to see
> That Love's a *Motion Natural* to Me.

The 'I' of the opening lines, rhythmically and syntactically dominant, has become the passive agent of a protracted motion and, since he has so completely surrendered his autonomy, the lover's protests seem gratuitous in retrospect. Donne's rakish lyrics sustain to the end their 'hyperbole above reason'; it is this hyperbole which codes them for us, which ensures the rake's freedom from commitment and the pleasure we take in such freedom. But the code will not work for Cowley, any more than the ritualised plaint of Elizabethan lyric.

IV

Even though the codes no longer resonate, the positions they have prepared are still available, untenanted structures ready for occupation. People are still likely to write poems where the mistress is the locus of paradox, and poems where the lover is the locus of paradox; the problem is that these poems no longer communicate so confidently about their own communications, they no longer say 'this is ritual' or 'this is a *jeu d'esprit*'. To put it another way, there is no longer any distance between the levels of statement within a poem, between message (Why has Astraea rejected my gift of bath-salts?) and code (this is a ritual which every lover has to endure). The absence or relative unobtrusiveness of this second level produces the kind of curiously flat poem which abounds in *The Mistress*, statements which might or might not be taken literally.

The relation between subject and object established by Donne's rakish lyrics was appropriated by later poets, but without his marvellous control of tone and false logic we have nothing to tell us 'this is a game' and the result is often one-dimensional: cynicism or ugly contempt. John Cleveland's 'A young Man to an old Woman Courting him', for example, places the lover in a position of absolute dominance over his mistress:

> My moderne lips know not (alack)
> The old Religion of thy smack.
> I count that primitive embrace,
> As out of fashion as thy face.
> And yet so long 'tis since thy fall,
> Thy Fornication's Classicall.

Cleveland's tone is that of a man confident that the intellectual terms of trade have been securely adjusted in his favour. This security depends on the establishment of a boundary—an absolute distinction—between self and other, between 'My moderne lips' and the 'old Religion of thy smack'; a boundary which by its very placement determines the superiority of self over other, modern over ancient. Cleveland's most brutally effective poems, such as 'The Rebell Scot', deal with situations which require the drawing of a line between 'us' and 'them', and the subsequent denigration of whatever lies on the other side of that line. This technique is no dramatic propriety, but rather an effect integral to Cleveland's verse, which takes a grip on experience from outside, its *point d'appui* often the specialist term introduced into a line as rhyme-word:

> So 'tis not her the Bee devours,
> It is a pretty maze of flowers;
> It is the rose that bleeds when he
> Nibbles his nice Phlebotomy.

The poet is distinguished from the woman by his possession of a specific vocabulary, which he uses as an instrument of control rather than as a means of self-expression. His language marks him as the man-who-knows, powerful because expert. The Restoration rake added sexuality to this conjunction of power and knowledge, so that sexual knowledge, enabling the alteration or even violation of another person, became an important mode of self-assertion. Rochester, for example, was systematic in this, as the first two stanzas of the lyric 'Love and Life' demonstrate:

> All my past life is mine no more;
>   The flying hours are gone,
> Like transitory dreams given o'er
> Whose images are kept in store
>   By memory alone.
>
> Whatever is to come is not:
>   How can it then be mine?
> The present moment's all my lot,
> And that, as fast as it is got,
>   Phyllis, is wholly thine.

These stanzas recapitulate a passage from Hobbes's account of memory in *Leviathan*: 'The *present* only has a being in nature; things *past* have a being in the memory only, but things *to come* have no being at all; the *future* being but a fiction of the mind, applying the sequels of actions past, to the actions that are present; which with most certainty is done by him that has most experience, but not with certainty enough'. By adducing a factual account of the way the mind works, Rochester was able to place the traditional persuasion to enjoy the moment on a systematic basis. It is the possession of (specialist) knowledge which gives him power over his mistress and, as with Cleveland, the exercise of control over people is also a matter of poetic technique:

> Let the porter and the groom,
>   Things designed for dirty slaves,
> Drudge in fair Aurelia's womb
>   To get supplies for age and graves.[11]

The pronounced metrical stress on 'Drudge' is precisely the stress or pressure of the poet's contempt, as he draws the line between himself and 'the porter and the groom', reducing everyone on the other side of that line to a thing. There had of course been poets before Cleveland and Rochester who addressed straightforwardly domineering or derogatory poems to their mistresses. But here the signs of the superiority of lover over mistress—caustic wit, mastery of a specialist knowledge unavailable to the lady, mastery of form—are not so much a coding ('this is play', 'this is collective rage') as a fixing of positions, a 'realism'. It is only too easy, in my view, for the reader to mistake code for message, metacommunication for communication—a mistake often made by participants in play and ritual. Bateson's example of monkeys playing makes this clear. The playful nip one monkey gives the other denotes a bite—involves the same actions as biting—but it does not denote what would normally be denoted by a bite (hostility); it is not 'meant' as a bite. But the other monkey may ignore or mistake its coding as 'nip' rather than 'bite', think he is being attacked and respond accordingly. Similarly, in the Andaman Islands, peace is concluded after each side has been given ceremonial freedom to strike the other. But if the discrimination between communication (I am about to hit you) and metacommunication (this is ritual) fails, if the ritual blows of peace-making are mistaken for the 'real' blows of combat, then the peace-making ceremony becomes a battle.[12] Poetry is more complicated in that the communications involved (the equivalent of bite or real blow) are themselves fictional; however mistaken we are, we cannot very well respond by punching Cleveland in the mouth. Even so, I think that Cleveland's poems allow us to mistake 'nip' for 'bite', playful disdain for sadism, in a way in which the more carefully coded poems of Donne do not; their frame, Bateson would say, is more labile. It is not a matter of mistaking fiction for life, the opinions of a narrative persona for those of Cleveland himself; but rather of mistaking one kind of fictional statement for another, fictional 'nip' for fictional 'bite'. Rochester's lyrics, like his satires, also permit such confusion, although they are more knowingly playful and their coding does not fail so often.

Cowley was not able, as I have pointed out, to sustain the relation of superiority constructed by the coding of Donne's rakish lyrics and 'taken literally' by Cleveland and Rochester; there can be no question, in *The Mistress*, of playful disdain modulating into sadism. Rather, it is the relation of *inferiority* constructed by Elizabethan lyric which becomes literal, 'real' combat rather than ritual. In order to explain this process of becoming literal, I want to draw on an approach to the problem of 'schizophrenia' also developed by Bateson. In doing so I do not intend any comment on the therapeutic validity of that approach or on Cowley's mental condition; I use it because it seems to me to offer an explanation of the way in which a failure of coding fixes those who suffer it in the positions proscribed for them and restricts them to a certain kind of language. According to Bateson, 'schizophrenia' is not a disease, a division within the mind of the patient, so much as a problem of communication among the members of a social group (usually the family). It constitutes a defensive reaction on the part of one member of the group in the face of paradoxical communications from another member. Each paradoxical communication has the effect, on the 'victim', of what has been termed a 'double bind'. A double bind may operate in a situation where two or more people are involved in an intense relationship:

In such a context, a message is given which is so structured that (a) it asserts something, (b) it asserts something about its own assertion and (c) these two assertions are mutually exclusive.

Thus, if the message is an injunction, it must be disobeyed to be obeyed; if it is a definition of self or the other, the person thereby defined is this kind of person only if he is not, and is not if he is. The meaning of the message is, therefore, undecidable . . .

The recipient of the message cannot step outside the frame set up by the message, either by commenting on it—since it is neither true nor false, but undecidable—or by avoiding it—since the relationship it presupposes is so intensely meaningful for him. 'Therefore, even though the message is logically meaningless, it is a pragmatic reality: he cannot *not* react to it, but neither can he react to it appropriately (nonparadoxically), for the message itself is paradoxical.'[13]

Cowley defines his relationship to his 'mistress' as a similar 'double bind'. Because that relationship is assumed to be intense, her every act has meaning for him; he cannot not react to it. But her behaviour is so paradoxical that he cannot make sense of it. She seems to assert two things at once, and he never knows which to believe:

> What new found *Rhetorick* is thine?
>   Ev'n thy *Diswasions* me *perswade*,
> And thy great power does clearest shine,
>   When thy *Commands* are *disobey'd*.
> In vain thou bidst me to forbear;
> *Obedience* were *Rebellion* here.   (P, 95)

Relationship involves the sending and receiving of messages: rhetoric, persuasion, injunction. But the mistress's rhetoric is paradoxical; it contains mutually exclusive assertions. Thus, perhaps, what she says persuades him to one course of action, while the way she says it persuades him to another, contradictory course. Her 'great power' must be disobeyed in order to be obeyed; obedience is disobedience. This type of double bind is described most explicitly in 'The Innocent Ill':

> Though all thy gestures and discourses be
>   Coyn'd and stamp't by *Modestie*,
>   Though from thy *Tongue* ne're slipt away
> One word which *Nuns* at th' *Altar* might not say,

> Yet such a sweetness, such a grace
>   In all thy *speech* appear,
>   That what to th' *Eye* a beauteous *face*,
>   That thy *Tongue* is to th' *Ear*.
> So cunningly its wounds the heart,
> It strikes such heat through every part,
> That thou a *Tempter* worse than Satan art.   (P, 145)

The mistress's communications, her 'gestures and discourses', are chaste in content, without a single word 'which *Nuns* at th' *Altar* might not say'. Yet their 'sweetness' and 'grace', the tone in which they are spoken, ensure that they have an entirely opposite, inflammatory effect. The problem for the lover is to decide which order of message is *really meant*, since they appear to be mutually exclusive. Does she mean to attract or to repel?

> Though in thy thoughts scarce any Tracks have bin
>   So much as of *Original* Sin,
>   Such charms thy *Beauty* wears as might
> Desires in dying confest *Saints* excite.
>   Thou with strange *Adulterie*
>   Dost in each breast a *Brother keep*;
>   *Awake* all men do *lust* for thee,
>   And some *enjoy* Thee when they *sleep*.

Johnson considered these lines 'indelicate and disgusting', and it is certainly true that, as the lover becomes more and more frustrated at his inability to say which order of message is really meant, so the vehemence and extravagance of his imagery increases. For the paradoxical injunction of the double bind '*bankrupts choice itself*, nothing is possible, and a self-perpetuating oscillating series is set in motion'.[14] Cowley can do no more than perpetuate his own bafflement:

> Thou *lovely Instrument* of *angry Fate*,
>   Which *God* did for our faults create!
>   Thou *Pleasant, Universal Ill*,
> Which *sweet* as *Health*, yet like a *Plague* dost *kill*!
>   Thou kind, well-natur'ed *Tyrannie*!
>   Thou *chast* committer of a *Rape*!
>   Thou *voluntary Destinie*,

Which no man *Can*, or *Would* escape!
So gentle, and so glad to spare,
So wondrous good, and wondrous fair,
(We know) e'ven the *Destroying Angels* are.   (P, 146)

Each paradox oscillates between contradictory but equally compelling signs; even theology offers no escape from paradox, because it is itself founded on paradox. God inflicts on man
punishments such as the plague, but these punishments are
(paradoxically) a sign of his love: 'My son, despise not the chas-
tening of the Lord; neither be weary of his correction: For whom
the Lord loveth he correcteth; even as a father the son in whom he
delighteth' (Proverbs 3, 11–12). The problem for both son and
believer is to decide whether the chastisement is vengeful (a sign of
hate) or corrective (a sign of love), 'bite' or 'nip'. Cowley does not
use theological metaphor to comment on or place human experience; believer and lover find themselves in the same situation, because both are subjected to double binds, and the terms in which
they account for that situation are therefore equivalent. That is
why Cowley's critics were so disturbed by the incidence of theological metaphor in *The Mistress*. Henry Stubbe, attacking the
immorality encouraged by the activities of the Royal Society,
singled out the collection: 'If any one would understand, what is
particularly meant by this application of *Sacred Writ* to vulgar
discourse, and the manner of this *Holy Raillery* deduced from *Scripture*: let him read Mr. *Cowley's* Poems, especially his *Mistresse*'.
Stubbe objected to the use of 'Scripture-expressions' out of context, as morally neutral figures of speech representing psychological states, and he cited examples from 'Resolv'd to be
beloved', 'The Welcome', and 'My Fate'. Edmund Elys, too, ful-
minated against the equivalence of sacred text with the language
of love. 'What *Prophaneness* also', he wrote, 'is this Author guilty of,
who uses these Sacred Words, HEAVEN, DEITY, DIVINE PRESENCE,
FAITH, &c. to set forth his *Dissolute* Amorous Conceptions.'.[15]
Cowley's account of his relation to a 'mistress' employs two lan-
guages, 'Amorous Conceptions' and 'Sacred Words', without distinguishing between them, without coding them adequately.
Poems like 'The Innocent Ill' describe the inability of a lover to
decide which of two contradictory signs is actually meant, and
they pass on this confusion to the reader by failing to code their
metaphors. Elys and Stubbe may well have been unusually obtuse

men, but it does not surprise me that they took Cowley's theological metaphors literally, mistaking (if that is what they did) fictional 'nip' for fictional 'bite'; Cowley himself sowed the seeds of confusion.

Joseph Addison, in his perceptive account of the language of *The Mistress*, isolated a species of 'mixt wit' as its defining characteristic. Whereas 'true wit consists in the resemblance of ideas, and false wit in the resemblance of words', mixt wit 'consists partly in the resemblance of ideas and partly in the resemblance of words'. True wit discerns a surprising congruity between dissimilar concepts. These concepts remain distinct in the reader's mind, as vehicle and tenor, the wit residing in the form of relationship established. Addison's 'true wit' would thus appear to conform to the literary practice defined by Rosemond Tuve in her analysis of the logical bases of Elizabethan and Metaphysical imagery. The category of 'mixt wit' was first proposed by Addison in the course of his notes on Ovid's *Metamorphoses*:

> When in two Ideas that have some resemblance with each other, and are both expressed by the same word, we make use of the ambiguity of the word to speak that of one Idea included under it, which is proper to the other. Thus, for example, most languages have hit on the word, which properly signifies Fire, to express Love by, (and therefore we may be sure there is some resemblance in the Ideas mankind have of them;) from hence the witty Poets of all languages, when they have once called Love a fire, consider it no longer as the passion, but speak of it under the notion of a real fire, and, as the turn of wit requires, make the same word in the same sentence stand for either of the Ideas that is annexed to it. . . . I should not have dwelt so long on this instance, had it not been so frequent in *Ovid*, who is the greatest admirer of this mixt wit of all the Ancients, as our Cowley is among the Moderns.

Mixt wit *identifies* love with fire, abstract with concrete, so that it is spoken of not as a passion but as a 'real fire'. There is no distance between vehicle and tenor, no congruity asserted on the basis of certain specified attributes only. Thus, one word ('flame', for example) might in the same sentence stand for 'either of the Ideas that is annexed to it'. When Addison came to reformulate the concept of mixt wit for his *Spectator* essay, he claimed that it 'abounds in Cowley, more than in any author that ever wrote', and produced sixteen examples from *The Mistress* to prove his point. His contention, which seems to me irrefutable, is that Cowley identifies love with fire, treating it not as a passion but as a 'real fire': 'When it does not let him sleep, it is a flame that sends up no smoke; when it is opposed by counsel and advice, it is a fire that rages the more by the wind's blowing upon it'.[16]

Addison remarked that Spenser, Milton, Dryden and Boileau had all ignored the device of mixt wit, but that Waller had 'a great deal of it', thus locating it in history at the moment of the exhaustion of a particular discourse. I would argue that mixt wit was produced at that moment by a failure of coding which left the poet unable to say what kind of poem he was writing; it was a scrambled code, neither one thing nor the other, which passed the responsibility for 'making sense' over to the reader. In this respect, Addison's account of Cowley's practice in *The Mistress* conforms to modern discussions of 'schizophrenic' discourse. 'In schizophrenia', Freud wrote,

> words are subject to the same process as that which makes the dream-images out of latent dream-thoughts—they undergo condensation, and by means of displacement transfer their cathexes to one another in their entirety. The process may go so far that a single word, if it is especially suitable on account of its numerous connections, takes over the representation of a whole train of thought.

One might note first of all that, according to Addison, the Latin poets employed mixt wit 'in their descriptions of Pictures, Images, Dreams, Apparitions, Metamorphoses, and the like'; it seemed particularly appropriate to the ambiguous borderline between fantasy and reality. In mixt wit, as in the language of schizophrenia, words 'transfer their cathexes to one another *in their entirety*', so that they become completely identified, and 'a single word' (fire) may take over 'the representation of a whole train of thought' (love). Witty poets, as Addison put it, 'when they have once called Love a fire, consider it no longer as the passion, but speak of it under the notion of a real fire'. The logic of this identification has been defined by Von Domarus as a deviance in syllogistic structure. Whereas the logician accepts identity of propositions only upon the basis of identical subjects, the schizophrenic (or 'paralogician') accepts identity based upon identical predicates. Thus, in the syllogism 'All men are mortal; Socrates is a man; Socrates is mortal', the identical concept is the subject 'man'; Socrates is mortal because he is a man. An example of the identity of predicates would be the basic similitude discussed by Addison: Fire burns; love 'burns'; love is a fire—an identification made from what can be said about the concepts of fire and love, from a single common predicate. One of Von Domarus's patients believed that Jesus, cigar boxes, and sex were identical, because the head of Jesus is encircled by a halo, the package of cigars by the tax band, and the woman by the 'sex glance' of the man; they could be identified by the single common predicate of 'being surrounded'. But this is only a way of saying that the thought of schizophrenics, like mixt wit, is rich in metaphor, as are many forms of thought and of wit. Donne, for example, saw the congruity between what could be said about lovers and what could be said about compasses. The difference is that he did not act as though lovers and compasses were the same thing, but rather maintained a certain distance between tenor and vehicle. 'The peculiarity of the schizophrenic', Bateson points out, 'is not that he uses metaphors, but that he uses *unlabelled* metaphors'. He confuses the literal and the metaphorical, 'bite' and 'nip', in such a way that it is impossible to tell which is which, thus passing his own inability to make that distinction on to the listener. He never gives any indication as to how his statements are to be interpreted. Similarly, mixt wit elides tenor and vehicle, making 'the same word in the same sentence stand for either of the Ideas that is annexed to it'. In the world of mixt wit, the passion of love is treated as a 'real fire'; like the world of the schizophrenic, that of *The Mistress* is 'pathologically concrete and void of abstract interpretation'.[17] Abstract and concrete, word and thing become identified, and the result for the reader, who is rarely told how to respond, can be confusing. Criticising *The Mistress*, Johnson referred to Addison's concept of mixt wit, 'which consists of thoughts true in one sense of the expression, and false in the other', and then went on to describe Addison's assessment as 'too indulgent' and to condemn the whole 'confusion of images'. The 'schizophrenic' victim of a double bind has precisely this (insoluble) problem of deciding in what 'sense of the expression' a communication may be meant, and will translate this bewilderment into riddling messages that may well strike others as a 'confusion of images'.

Perhaps the best example of mixt wit in *The Mistress*, one noted by Addison, is 'The Tree':

1

> I chose the flouri'shingst *Tree* in all the Park,
>   With freshest Boughs, and fairest head;
> I cut my Love into his gentle Bark,
>   And in three days, behold, 'tis *dead*;
> My very *written flames* so vi'olent be
>   They 'have burnt and wither'd up the Tree: (P, 140)

This stanza has the tone of a folk-tale: the three superlatives in the opening lines, the jaunty narrative ('I chose . . . I cut . . .'), the ballad-like alternation of long and short lines. It deals with the effect of an action on the natural world, but that action has clearly overstepped the limits of the familiar or empirically observable. The practice of inscribing names on trees was customary enough, in verse at least:

> My songs they be of *Cynthia's* praise,
> I weare her Rings on Holy dayes,
> In every Tree I write her name,
> And every Day I read the same.

But if Cynthia should ask for her rings back, Greville continues, 'I blot her name out of the Tree'.[18] Cowley's action, on the other hand, is not so easily reversible; it has set in motion the altogether different logic of mixt wit. His love is both a passion and a 'real fire', and therefore burns the tree. The problem, posed by the interpolated 'behold', is to decide what this strange event might mean. How, and to whom, is the violence unleashed by the '*written flames*' directed? The poet's thoughts, naturally enough, rebound onto himself:

2

> How should I live my self, whose *Heart* is found
>   Deeply graven every where
> With the large *History* of many a *wound*,
>   Larger than thy *Trunk* can bear?
> With art as strange, as *Homer* in the *Nut*,
>   *Love* in my *Heart* has *Volumes* put.

The implications of this violence are potentially disastrous, since he is himself so deeply 'graven' with written flames. He cannot, that is to say, afford to ignore the significance of the burnt tree; he finds himself faced by a problem which he can either solve or succumb to, but never avoid. This stanza simply emphasises the depth and the strangeness of his implication in the search for a 'solution'. The first stanza had described the effect of an action on nature, the second stresses the significance of this effect for the poet, and this alternation of external and internal is continued by the third and fourth stanzas:

3

What a few words from thy rich stock did take
    The *Leaves* and *Beauties* all?
As a strong *Poyson* with one *drop* does make
    The *Nails* and *Hairs* to fall:
Love (I see now) a kind of *Witchcraft* is,
    Or *Characters* could ne're do this.

4

Pardon ye *Birds* and *Nymphs* who lov'd this *Shade*;
    And pardon me, thou gentle *Tree*;
I thought her *name* would thee have happy made,
    And blessed *Omens* hop'd from Thee;
Notes of my *Love*, thrive here (said I) and *grow*;
    And with ye let my *Love* do so.

The third stanza pursues the strange withering of the tree by folk-tale allusions to poison and witchcraft, while the fourth contrasts with this sinister violence the innocence of the poet's motive. He is an innocent in search of 'blessed *Omens*' who encounters only violent unintelligibility, a lack of explicit meaning he can neither transcend nor avoid. For Cowley, this conflict between innocence of motive and unintelligibility of effect characterises the lover's situation and, as in 'The Prophet' and 'My Dyet', the assertive *subject* of the opening stanza becomes an *object* of pity:

5

Alas poor youth, thy love will never thrive!
    This blasted *Tree Predestines* it;

> Go tye the dismal *Knot* (why shouldst thou live?)
>   And by the Lines thou there hast writ
> Deform'dly hanging, the *sad Picture* be
>   To that unlucky *History*.

Sidney's coding of the lover's plight—'I am not I, pitie the tale of
me'—will have to be rewritten as 'I am not the tale, pity me for my
literalness'. The wounds ritually graven on the lover's body as a
kind of collective memory, a continually reinvented tale, have
been inflicted in earnest this time. 'The metaphors are not meta-
phoric' is the metaphor on which the poem is based; its fiction
states that the fiction is truth. As Bateson says of 'schizophrenic'
discourse, the 'indication that it is a metaphorical statement lies
in the fantastic aspect of the metaphor, not in the signals which
usually accompany metaphors to tell the listener that a metaphor
is being used'.[19] 'The Tree' is not coded as any particular kind of
metaphor, and we are therefore left to make what sense we can of
its 'fantastic aspect', its mixt wit.

Cowley himself described the experience of this fantastic literalness in a poem called 'The Dissembler', where the lover complains
that what he intended as a mock-declaration of love has become
the real thing:

2

> I thought, I'll swear, an handsome ly
> Had been no *sin* at all in *Poetry*:
>   But now I suffer an *Arrest*,
>   For words were spoke by me in *jest*.
> Dull, sottish *God* of *Love*, and can it be
>   Thou understand'st not *Raillery*?

3

> *Darts*, and *Wounds*, and *Flame*, and *Heat*,
> I nam'd but for the *Rhime*, or the *Conceit*.
>   Nor meant my Verse should raised be,
>   To this sad fame of *Prophesie*;
> *Truth* gives a *dull propriety* to my stile,
>   And all the *Metaphors* does spoil.   (P, 132)

Even the God of Love, it would seem, does not have a perfect ear
for the coding of statements as '*Raillery*'; even he occasionally mis-

takes 'nip' for 'bite'. The *jeu d'esprit* has been taken seriously, the metaphors have been spoilt. Ironically, this poem, which announces the supersession of fiction by truth, is itself based on a literary model, an already institutionalised fiction. It recapitulates Ovid's warning, in the *Ars Amatoria*, that the dissembler may start to love truly and thus become what he has pretended to be:

> Saepe tamen vere coepit simulator amare,
> Saepe, quod incipiens finxerat esse, fuit.

Forty lines later, arguing that those who contrive instruments of exploitation deserve to be the first to suffer by them, Ovid cites the example of Phalaris and Perillus. Perillus made for Phalaris an artificial bull and was then burnt alive inside it:

> Et Phalaris tauro violenti membra Perilli
> Torruit: infelix inbuit auctor opus.
> ... neque enim lex aequior ulla est,
> Quam necis artifices arte perire sua.[20]

Concluding his poem, Cowley uses the same example to describe how the dissembler has been overcome by weapons of his own contriving:

> But now, by *Love*, the mighty *Phalaris*, I
> My *burning Bull* the first do try.

Thus the two major exponents of mixt wit fictionalise that becoming literal of discourse which spoils their metaphors for them.

V

It would, however, be wrong to suppose that *The Mistress* is entirely preoccupied with the failure of codes and the consequences of that failure. The collection does include poems which follow conventions usually thought of as 'Cavalier' and which solve the problem of fixation. John Oldmixon remarked that in *The Mistress* Cowley had copied Donne's faults, 'and it seems strange to me, that after *Suckling* and *Waller* had written, whose Genius's were so fine and just, Mr. *Cowley* should imitate Dr. *Donne*; in whom there's hardly any Thing that's agreeable, or one Stroke which has any Likeness to Nature'.[21] But Cowley was well aware of what '*Suckling* and *Waller* had written'. In 'The Given Love' he promised to fix his mistress's name next to that of Sacharissa, the recipient of Waller's love-verses, and he was also influenced by Suckling, whose *Fragmenta Aurea*, published posthumously in 1646, contained most of the secular poetry he had written during the 1630s. One might compare Suckling's 'Loving and Beloved' with Cowley's 'Resolved to Love', which, as well as using the same stanza-form, arrives in its concluding verse at a scepticism not dissimilar to Suckling's. Cowley's 'Against Fruition' borrows some material from Suckling's 'Against Fruition (2)' which was published in *Fragmenta Aurea* and had already appeared in slightly different form as a dialogue between Samantha and Orithie in *Aglaura* (1638), Act I, Scene v. He was clearly familiar with the Cavalier mode, and his most impressive poem in this mode was 'The Waiting-Maid':

1

Thy *Maid*? ah, find some nobler theame
   Whereon thy doubts to place;
Nor by a low suspect *blaspheme*
   The glories of thy face.

2

Alas, she makes Thee shine so fair,
   So exquisitely bright,
That her dim *Lamp* must disappear
   Before thy potent *Light*.

3

Three hours each morn in dressing Thee,
   Maliciously are spent;
And make that *Beauty Tyranny*,
   That's else a *Civil Government*.

4

The 'adorning thee with so much art,
   Is but a barb'arous skill;
'Tis like the *poys'oning* of a *Dart*
   Too apt before to kill.

5

> The *Min'istring Angels* none can see;
>   'Tis not their beauty 'or face,
> For which by men they worshipt be;
>   But their high *Office* and their *place.*
> *Thou* art my *Goddess*, my *Saint*, *She*;
> I pray to *Her*, only to pray to *Thee.*   (P, 138)

This poem is another example of the importance of Ovid for Cowley, deriving in fact from the *Amores* II, vii and II, viii. Ovid, too, complains that his mistress suspects him unjustly of having an affair with her maid:

> Ecce novum crimen! sollers ornare Cypassis
>   obicitur dominae contemerasse torum.
> di melius, quam me, si sit peccasse libido,
>   sordida contemptae sortis amica iuvet!
> quis Veneris famulae conubia liber inire
>   tergaque conplecti verbere secta velit?
> adde, quod ornandis illa est operata capillis
>   et tibi perdocta est grate ministra manu—
> scillicet ancillam, quae tam tibi fida, rogarem!

The tone of outraged innocence, and of contempt for the maid, is clearly the same in both poems. But Ovid, in his next poem, immediately flouts the reader's expectations, admitting what he had previously denied:

> Ponendis in mille modos perfecta capillis,
>   comere sed solas digna, Cypassi, deas,
> et mihi iucundo non rustica cognita furto,
>   apta quidem dominae, sed magis apta mihi—
> quis fuit inter nos sociati corporis index?[22]

Some of these details—the maid's skill ('The 'adorning thee with so much art'), her ability to attend 'goddesses', the term 'apt'— find their way into Cowley's poem. But whereas Ovid is ostensibly concerned with the success or failure of his love in physical terms, Cowley focuses on the witty implications of the maid's abilities:

> The'adorning thee with so much art,
>   Is but a barb'arous skill;
> 'Tis like the *poys'oning* of a *Dart*
>   Too apt before to kill.

Cowley puns on 'barb'arous' and, taking up Ovid's term, on 'apt' (able to, liable to). The stanza is beautifully economical and it is hardly surprising that Johnson should have used it as an example of the way in which a telling wit can be combined with ease and urbanity. 'Easy poetry', which the stanza exemplifies,

> is that in which natural thoughts are expressed without violence to the language. The discriminating character of ease consists principally in the diction, for all the poetry requires that the sentiments be natural. Language suffers violence by harsh or by daring figures, by transposition, by unusual acceptations of words, and by any licence, which would be avoided by a writer of prose. Where any artifice appears in the construction of the verse, that verse is no longer easy. Any epithet which can be ejected without diminution of the sense, any curious iteration of the same word, and all unusual, tho' not ungrammatical structure of speech, destroy the grace of easy poetry.[23]

Easy poetry, by refraining from violence to language, does no violence to the reader either. Ease of language codes the poem, presiding over the establishment of a new, more easeful relation between lover and mistress, who are usually placed in unmediated opposition by Cowley's lyrics:

> By repercussion *Beams* engender *Fire*,
>   *Shapes* by reflexion *shapes* beget;
> The *voyce* it self, when stopt, does back retire,
>   And a new *voice* is made by it.
>   Thus things by *opposition*
> The gainers grow; my barren *Love* alone,
>   Does from her stony breast rebound,
> Producing neither *Image, Fire*, nor *Sound*.   (P, 108)

This total absence of response leaves the lover with two possible courses of action. He can either identify himself completely with the wishes of his mistress, making himself exactly what she wants him to be, as the slave identifies with his overseer, servant with master, prisoner with goaler; or he can withdraw into himself, and deny his own desire. However, he might be able to salve his anguish if he could find some way of mediating the opposition between self and other; if he could learn to regard his mistress as approachable *and* distant. Theology poses similar problems, for, however logical, the remoteness of a God who is the binary antithesis of man, inhabiting a world apart, may prove emotionally disturbing. Hence the need to reestablish a continuum by devising ambiguous beings—such as the virgin mother—who mediate between God and man, and themselves become objects of intense interest, as sacred as the gods themselves. Ovid devotes considerable attention to waiting-maids in the *Ars Amatoria* and the *Amores*, precisely because they are mediating figures, close to their mistresses but also a means of access for the lover. Cowley simply translates Ovid's preoccupation with intrigue into theological terms. His mistress is a '*Goddess*', her maid an officiating '*Saint*': 'I pray to *Her*, only to pray to *Thee*'. I would suggest that the ease of the poem derives from its discovery of a mediating factor. Just as Cowley has created in this instance a secular version of pre-Reformation theology, with its emphasis on the sacredness of mediation,[24] so the majority of his lyrics might be said to correspond to the theologies which replaced it: the distant and fearsome God of the English Puritans, the *Deus absconditus* of the Jansenists.

4 Cowley and Crashaw

In the previous chapter I examined *The Mistress* as a relatively autonomous work of literature, trying to offer an 'inside view' of the failure of certain codes. But because the love-lyric was a privileged form, the subject it made a place for—'I am not I, pitie the tale of me'—was always already the subject required by the operation of locutionary truth, the 'person propounding' whose every message reinvents a code we recognise and credit. If *The Mistress* appears morbid, it is because its ceaseless reproduction in a damaged state of that lyric subject must automatically be a comment on the increasing difficulty of sustaining a locutionary truth. The demise it meditates so extensively is obscurely felt to be that of a whole manner of speaking.

By the time Cowley came to write the Preface to the 1656 edition of his *Poems* he was better able to describe to himself and to his readers what had happened. He talked there about the need for poetry to redefine its function. The Preface apologises for *The Mistress* but invests heavily in the seriousness of the *Davideis*, Cowley's unfinished epic about the life of David; it builds up to an emotional plea for the transformation of poetry from a profane to a sacred art. This transformation, he says, would involve the abandonment of appealing falsehood and a renewed devotion to literal truth:

> There is not so great a *Lye* to be found in any *Poet*, as the vulgar conceit of men, that *Lying* is *Essential* to good *Poetry*. Were there never so wholesome *Nourishment* to be had (but alas, it breeds nothing but *Diseases*) out of these boasted *Feasts* of *Love* and *Fables*; yet, methinks, the unalterable continuance of the *Diet* should make us *Nauseate* it: For it is almost impossible to serve

up any *new Dish* of that kind . . . though those mad stories of the
Gods and *Heroes*, seem in themselves so ridiculous; yet they were
then the *whole Body* (or rather *Chaos*) of the *Theologie* of those
times. They were believed by all but a few *Philosophers*, and perhaps some *Atheists*, and served to good purpose among the
vulgar, (as pitiful things as they are) in strengthening the authority of *Law* with the terrors of *Conscience*, and expectation of certain rewards, and unavoidable punishments. There was no
other *Religion*, and therefore *that* was better than *none at all*. But
to us who have no need of them, to us who deride their *folly*, and
are wearied with their *impertinencies*, they ought to appear no
better arguments for *Verse*, then those of their worthy *Successors*,
the *Knights Errant*.   (P, 13–14)

Mythology ('those mad stories of the *Gods* and *Heroes* . . . the *whole
Body* (or rather *Chaos*) of the *Theologie* of those times') is an important instance of locutionary truth, where the credibility of the tale
depends completely on the strength of customary beliefs, on the
capacity of the 'person propounding' to reinvent a traditional
code. 'A *mythos*', Jane Harrison wrote, 'to the Greeks was primarily just a thing spoken, uttered by the *mouth* . . . From sounds
made by the mouth, to words spoken and thence to tale or story
told the transition is easy'.[1] During the 1640s Cowley, Hobbes
and Davenant came to agree that myth ought no longer to be considered suitable subject-matter for poetry, which should henceforth concern itself with 'men and manners' rather than with
fables depending on 'faith in men only'; a resolution which co-
incided with the emergence in the work of Hobbes of the alternative
criterion of propositional truth. Cowley first stated his view of the
matter in an occasional poem, 'To Sir William Davenant. Upon
his two first Books of *Gondibert*, finished before his voyage to
America':

> Methinks *Heroick Poesie* till now
> Like some fantastick *Fairy Land* did show,
> *Gods, Devils, Nymphs, Witches* and *Gyants race*,
> And all but *Man* in *Mans chief work* had place.
> Thou like some worthy *Knight* with sacred Arms
> Dost drive the *Monsters* thence, and end the *Charms*.
> Instead of those dost *Men* and *Manners* plant,
> The things which that rich *Soil* did chiefly want.   (P, 42)

Here he seems to countenance the kind of fable found in the epics of Tasso and Spenser: worthy knights dispelling charms and monsters by force of 'sacred Arms'. But by the Preface to the 1656 *Poems* his attitude had hardened to exclude these fables of '*Knights Errant*' (as, of course, Milton was to do in Book IX of *Paradise Lost*). His own contribution to post-mythological poetry was the *Davideis*, which boldly proclaims that 'Truth is *truest Poesie*' (P, 243).

But how does this Truth manifest itself in poetry? Is not epic poetry by definition a medium of locutionary truth and therefore implicated in the demise of mythology? I shall return to these problems in the next chapter, when I come to talk about the *Davideis*, but it seems to me that the solution offered by the *Preface* is ambiguous:

> It is not without grief and indignation that I behold that *Divine Science* employing all her inexhaustible riches of *Wit* and *Eloquence*, either in the wicked and beggerly *Flattery* of great persons, or the unmanly *Idolizing* of *Foolish Women*, or the wretched affectation of scurril *Laughter*, or at best on the confused antiquated *Dreams* of senseless *Fables* and *Metamorphoses*. Amongst all holy and consecrated things which the *Devil* ever stole and alienated from the service of the *Deity*; as *Altars, Temples, Sacrifices, Prayers*, and the like; there is none that he so universally, and so long usurpt, as *Poetry*. It is time to recover it out of the *Tyrants* hands, and to restore it to the *Kingdom* of *God*, who is the *Father* of it. It is time to *Baptize* it in *Jordan*, for it will never become clean by bathing in the *Water* of *Damascus*.   (P, 13)

If pressed, Cowley would surely have had to admit that *The Mistress* included its fair share of 'unmanly *Idolizing* of *Foolish Women*'; he himself had known the exhaustion of the antiquated and corrupt poetic he now deplores, from the inside. This fabling poetic was to be superseded by a greater truthfulness: 'Truth is *truest Poesie*'. The problematising of locutionary truth evident in the mid-century disavowal of mythology required that more attention be paid to the 'propositional truth' of statements. But Cowley here describes poetry as a kind of sacred ritual which, like '*Altars, Temples, Sacrifices, Prayers*', has been perverted to evil ends: as a medium of locutionary truth which far from being demystified is to be put through further, intensified ritual ('It is time to *Baptize* it in *Jordan*'). One criterion of truth was, gradually and unevenly, being replaced by another and people represented this change to themselves in contradictory ways: sometimes as the replacement of superstition and mythology by real knowledge; sometimes as the replacement of one (incredible) myth by another (credible) myth. Cowley's involvement in this process of redefinition was catalysed and to some extent determined by his encounter with Richard Crashaw.

II

Cowley entered Trinity College, Cambridge, in 1636, already with a literary reputation, and it was probably in response to the third edition of *Poeticall Blossoms*, a collection of juvenilia reprinted in 1637, that Crashaw wrote his 'Upon two greene Apricockes sent to Cowley by Sir Crashaw':

> O had my wishes
> And the deare merits of your Muse, their due,
> The yeare had found some fruit early as you;
> Ripe as those rich composures time computes
> Blossoms, but our blest tast confesses fruits.[2]

The friendship begun in Cambridge was resumed later in Paris and proved remarkably durable, considering the variance of character and preoccupation. Crashaw's life moved along a single line, with one decisive change of direction; Cowley's, to judge by the instability of his political allegiance and his rather nondescript religious beliefs, was far less channelled. Whereas Crashaw lived and studied within the Laudian ambiance of Peterhouse, Cowley addressed a congratulatory poem to Laud's bitter enemy, Bishop Williams, 'Upon his Enlargement out of the Tower'. Libellous letters sent to Williams by Lambert Osbaldeston, one of Cowley's masters at Westminster, provided the main evidence at the second Star Chamber prosecution of the Bishop. Osbaldeston was condemned to the pillory, the loss of his living, and a fine of £5000, although he escaped before the sentence could be executed.[3] Cowley was, then, taking sides on a very controversial issue, against Laud. Furthermore, Crashaw's development as a poet has been described as a progress, 'hestitatingly, but with a felt sense of direction, from the epigram to the ode'. His practice involved the permutation of a limited number of images and rhyme pairs, each of which carried a dense symbolic reference.[4] Cowley, however, experimented with a wide variety of modes. When Crashaw composed irregular odes, he composed them in accordance with a religious ideal; Cowley, on the other hand, sensitive primarily to problems of intellectual procedure, developed a Pindaric form more closely related to the succession of ideas in the mind than to any devotional poetic. Indeed, his thought as a whole never followed a single path. 'This . . . is most remarkable', Sprat wrote, 'that a Man who was so constant and fix'd in the Moral Ideas of his mind, should yet be so changable in his Intellectual' (*Life*, W, Sig B2 recto). But this difference of character and literary preoccupation has a cultural basis, and to understand its significance one has to explore the context of their respective attitudes.

During the reign of Charles I, William Laud was responsible for an ambitious attempt to impose a uniform shape on the many conflicting forms of worship practised at the time. As Trevor-Roper puts it, he coordinated into a policy the protests of those disadvantaged by the emergence of a new social order, and ensured the cohesion of those protests by devising an 'appropriate religious doctrine'. It is that doctrine, and its extension into ceremonial practice, which will concern me here. Laud aimed to perpetuate a traditional social order by insisting on the minutiae of ceremonial observance; he countered the Puritan emphasis on individual conscience as the rule of faith—which falls into the category of 'propositional truth' because it claims that the truth of God's Word is self-evident, appearing to the believer without mediation—by encouraging an overtly gestural, spoken piety. Ceremony involves a sequence of events which are meaningless in themselves (without 'propositional content'), but which taken together sustain a social code; thus constituting a perpetually renewed tribal memory, a memory etched in the gestures and observances of the participants. As long as this memory continues to be renewed, the code reinvented by acts of collective worship, then the social order will survive unchanged. But the code must be apparent rather than hermetic (sectarian) if it is to embrace all men and women, and Laud was careful to define personal identity, not as individual self-determination, but as a knowledge of one's place in society: 'If any man be so addicted to his private, that he neglects the common State, he is void of the sense of piety, and wisheth peace and happiness to himself in vain. For whoever he be, he must live in the body of the Commonwealth, and in the body of the Church; and if their joints be out, and in trouble, how can he hope to live in "peace"?' Since it construed the sense of piety as public rather than private, Laudian theology worked in practice by the provision of sacred places where that piety could be manifested publicly. Laud believed strongly in the official, public consecration of churches, whereas the Puritans thought that the individual conscience consecrated any place in which it chose to exercise itself; indeed, he had a superstitious anxiety about the sin of sacrilege, and recorded in his diary the death of a prospector who had dug for saltpetre in a church at Brecknock.[5] He also reasserted the ritual function of the priest, as a mediator between God and man deriving his authority from above and not from the community. These matters had proved divisive since the Reformation, and Laud's policies were intended to reestablish a pre-Reformation system of worship.

One churchman promoted by Laud in the teeth of bitter opposition from Parliament was John Cosin, who displayed considerable zeal in the dissemination of Laudian doctrine, stressing the value of ceremony and of the priesthood. His *Collection of Private Devotions*, published in 1627, was a defence of traditional doctrine, designed

> to let the world understand that they who give it out, & accuse us here in ENGLAND to have set up a *New Church*, and a *New Faith*, to have abandoned *All the Ancient Formes of Piety and Devotion*, to have taken away all the *Religious Exercises and Prayers of our Forefathers*, to have despised *all the old Ceremonies*, & cast behinde us the *Blessed Sacraments of Christs Catholicke Church*: that these men doe little else but betray their owne infirmities, and have more violence and wil, than reason or judgment.

The purpose of ceremony was to ensure continuity with a traditional social and religious order, and the Puritans were understandably annoyed by Cosin's work, Prynne and Burton writing fiercely critical replies. Like Laud, Cosin argued that 'private holiness at home will not serve', and that worship was a form of social solidarity:

> For this same home-holiness that is neither seen nor heard,

surely there is some leaven of malignity in it; and He can no skill of it, likes it not, will therefore have it come forth, seen in the countenance, expressed in the view, heard in the voice, and not in the voice of the pulpit only, to come and hear a sermon preached, but in the voice of the choir too, of the whole congregation together, to come and with one heart and one mouth to set forth His most worthy praise.

Worship can be considered genuine only if acted and spoken, printed out in gesture and word, 'seen in the countenance, expressed in the view, heard in the voice', and the participants themselves are both code and message, sustaining and reinventing the system of belief which gives meaning to their gestures. The distinction between prayer and preaching reflects the difference between Arminian and Puritan doctrine: between a truth expressed in ritual and song, and a truth known by its separate enforcement on each individual conscience. Similarly, Cosin thought that the regular observance of sacred seasons constituted a part of moral law: 'And this is moral, that all things in the service of God must be done in order, not that every body should appoint a day by himself; and this is moral too, that obedience must be given to superiors in those things wherein they are superior'. He had, furthermore, a very precise idea of how such observance worked, arguing that by the designation of a particular day, 'there is no morality infused or brought upon the day itself, but a former morality only awakened and revived, which consisteth in a due obedience to God, and to the order of His Church, which is our superior in these cases'.[6] This awakening and revival of 'former morality' ceaselessly renews a tribal memory; the overtly coded ceremony fits the worshipper to the traditional order of things, and the regularity of observance immunises that order against change.

It was Cosin who, while in attendance on the King, presented to Charles a biblical Concordance designed and used by the religious community at Little Gidding.[7] This community, labelled the 'Arminian nunnery' by one Puritan pamphleteer, is an interesting if aberrant example of religious practice under Laud's regime. Nicholas Ferrar, the community's guiding spirit, had travelled in Italy, absorbing Counter-Reformation values, and Trevor-Roper describes the community as 'one of the most curious testimonies to the revulsion of feeling against the Reformation which had affected certain classes, and the romantic idealisation of certain practices'.[8] Crashaw frequently visited Little Gidding, participated in the vigils and watches, and became tutor to Ferrar Collett, Nicholas Ferrar's nephew. Laud was anxious to place his supporters in high positions not only within the Church, but also within the Universities. On 8 February 1634, Cosin was elected Master of Peterhouse College, Cambridge, and remained as such until he was ejected by a warrant from the Earl of Manchester dated 13 March 1643. During that time, he provided the college chapel with lavish decorations, introduced elements of ritual such as the burning of incense, and fined scholars for non-attendance at prayers. Cosin was Master of Peterhouse while Crashaw was a Fellow there, between 1635 and 1643.

Crashaw provided a commendatory poem for another manual of Laudian doctrine, Robert Shelford's *Five Pious and Learned Discourses*, published at Cambridge in 1635. Shelford's most significant 'discourse', from my point of view, is 'A Sermon of Gods House', which insists on the sacred nature of church-buildings. 'Open therefore all thy eyes', he wrote,

> the eyes of thy minde, and the eyes of thy body; the eyes of thy body to behold the outward beauty of this house in divine service, and the eyes of thy soul to behold the inward beauty of Gods holinesse, majesty, and greatnesse; and thou canst not choose but be reverent more then our usuall manner is.

Religion aligns internal and external conduct to one end. Thus, 'ceremonies and civilities to men, when they are applied to God, change their nature, and become holinesse'; exact observance— bowing to the altar, taking off ones hat—is an integral part of piety, because it prints out the tribal memory for all to see. By ritual participation, by keeping the feasts of the Church, the believer sustains and reinvents that memory, because 'they which come upon S. Stephens day, are in affection partakers of his martyrdome, and prepared for holy suffering'. He is both himself, an individual in a particular place at a particular time, and the martyr Stephen, a paradigm. Like Cosin, Shelford emphasised the need for a public expression of faith: "The people must not onely joyn with the minister in heart, but in voice too; because of all outward means this is most significant and effectuall, as being

the hearts eruption and interpreter'. The emphasis on gesture, as
the 'hearts eruption and interpreter', places Cosin's concept of
faith within the category of 'locutionary truth'. Piety depends, to
adapt Hobbes's terms, on the 'person propounding' rather than
the 'proposition itself', on gesture rather than doctrine. The result
of meticulous internal and external observance, Shelford wrote,
will be a 'sanctified attention'.[9]

Such was the theological ambiance in which Crashaw lived and
studied at Peterhouse. In December 1640, the Commons established a committee to investigate religious abuses, which arrived
in Cambridge the next year, and the agents of this committee
singled out Peterhouse as a centre of Laudian practices:

> The schollers in ye Colledge are exceedingly Imployed to learne
> pricksong to ye great losse of theire time & prejudice of their
> studdyes, and the preferments of the Colledge are cast upon
> them according to theire skill & proficiency therein [.] After the
> second yeare, the third part of Aquinas *Summes* is appointed to
> be read by them, that betimes they may suck in the doctrine of
> the Papists.

The college buildings, like the students, did not escape scrutiny:
'This Chappell since Dr Cosins was admitted master of ye Col-
ledge hath bene so dressed up and ordered soe Cerimoniously,
that it hath become ye gaze of ye University & a greate invitation to
strangers'. Among the Fellows of Peterhouse, Joseph Beaumont
and Richard Crashaw received particular attention. Beaumont
was said to have inveighed bitterly against Calvin, and, in an
address delivered on 5 November 1640, to have claimed that the
Scots were more wicked than the 'powder traitors'. Crashaw,

> in a speech made in that Colledge Chappell *Die Annunciationis*
> 1639 is credibly reported to have turned himselfe to ye picture of
> the Virgine Mary & to have used these words *Hanc adoramus,
> colamus hanc*. That is ye rather probable because his practises in
> little St Maryes, where he is Curat are superstitious.[10]

Crashaw remained at Peterhouse for two years after these accus-
ations were made, but throughout the 1630s he must have felt
increasing pressure to identify with one or other religious party.
Eventually, this led him to Catholicism, via a succession of sacred

places: Little St Mary's, Little Gidding, Loretto.

These years at Peterhouse did not only serve to persuade Crashaw, whose father after all was a militant Puritan, of the theological value of gesture. Joseph Beaumont, a Fellow there from 1636 to 1644, became a close friend of his, and this relationship added a further element to the set of cultural attitudes Crashaw was to bring to his encounter with Cowley. Jean Hagstrum has argued that one notion which received greater emphasis in the century of the baroque than in the Renaissance was that 'in the union of body and soul, picture and word, sense and intellect, there was some kind of interpenetration'. I think there is some justification of talking in similar terms of a baroque notion of personal relationship. Joseph Beaumont, in one of several poems about male companionship, wrote:

> Hast thou a Friend? whate'r thou hast,
> Thou hast compleatly double: cast
> Up thy account no more for One,
> Thy scant Identitie is gone:
>   Thou art thy Friend, & he
> By mutuall Faith transanimates with Thee.

Such a notion of friendship exceeds the Ciceronian ideal of candour and conviviality, and the intensity of the experience can only be compared to transanimation, the transfer of one soul into another body; friendship thus becomes a form of religious devotion or 'sanctified attention', of identity lost and then regained at a higher level of communion. Thomas Carre, whom Crashaw knew in Paris, provided, in an 'Anagramme' prefixed to the 1652 edition of Crashaw's *Sacred Poems*, the ultimate witty interpenetration:

> Was CAR then Crashawe; or WAS Crashawe CAR,
> Since both within one name combined are?
> Yes, Car's Crashawe, he Car; t'is love alone
> Which melts two harts, of both composing one.[11]

The anagram enacts the emotional interpenetration of friendship which melts two hearts into one, an interpenetration Cowley refers to in a poem in the *Miscellanies* entitled 'Friendship in Absence':

> *I'am* there with *Thee*, yet here with *Me thou* art,
> Lodg'd in each others heart.   (P, 27)

But there is no equivalent in Cowley's poem to the baroque emphasis on the *fluidity* of interpenetration and on the complete loss
of identity involved in the melting of hearts. Indeed, he ends up
contemplating the intact and unbreachable limits of his own self:

> And when no Art affords me help or ease,
> I seek with verse my griefs t'appease.
> Just as a *Bird* that flies about
> And beats it self against the *Cage*,
> Finding at last no passage out
> It sits, and sings, and so orecomes its rage.

Whereas Cowley returns to the fixity and solidity of selfhood,
Crashaw and Beaumont developed a poetic based on those gestures which obliterate selfhood, or which integrate selfhood into
the communion of the faithful.

The evidence for the development by Crashaw and Beaumont
of a devotional poetic lies in a source which so far has only been
used, by Warren and by Martin, to provide biographical infor-
mation—Canto IV of Beaumont's *Psyche*.[12] In this Canto, the
Senses rebel against Psyche, but inevitably start quarrelling
amongst themselves. Acoe (hearing), in response to a previous
effort by Opsis, produces, through the agency of Anamnesis
(memory), a pageant of the glories of poetry. Because this
pageant is clearly selective, it deserves some attention as the
possible basis of a poetic. The significance attached to the
great lyric poets extends Shelford's emphasis on the voice as
'the hearts eruption and interpreter'. As lyric poets, Pindar
and Horace are preeminent:

> But on the shore a singing Troop appear'd,
> Where *Pindar* first took up a Lute and plaid;
> All ears were ravish't which his Numbers heard,
> And had not *Flaccus*, though at first afraid,
>   Fir'd by a furious bravery stretch'd his skill,
>   *Pindar* had been sole *Lord of Lyrick* still.

A stanza introduced in the second edition of *Psyche* (1702) presented George Herbert as a worthy successor to Pindar and Horace:

> (Yet neither of their Empires was so vast
> But they left *Herbert* too full room to reign,
> Who Lyric's pure and precious Metal cast
> In holier moulds, and nobly durst maintain
>   *Devotion in Verse*, whilst by the spheres
>   He tunes his Lute, and plays to heav'nly ears.)[13]

The image of lyric poetry as molten metal cast in 'holier moulds' by Herbert is typically baroque, for liquidity, in Beaumont's figure, represents the loss of an identity which is restored after transformation at a higher level. This higher identity is the communion of the purified, and the means of its accomplishment '*Devotion in Verse*'.

Two stanzas acknowledge Beaumont's personal debt to Crashaw, and I shall quote as well the preceding stanza, which provides a context for that debt:

93

> But o, how low all these do bow before
> *Nazianzum's*, and the Worlds immortall Glory,
> Him, whose Heav'n-tuned soul did sweetly soar
> Unto the top of every stage and story
>   Of Poetry; through which, as hee did pass,
>   Hee all the *Muses* made *Urania's*.

94

> And by this soul-attracting Pattern, *Thou*,
> *My onely worthy self*, thy Songs didst frame:
> Witnesse those polish'd *Temple-Steps*, which now
> Whether thou wilt or no, this Truth proclaim,
>   And, spight of all thy Travels, make't appear
>   Th'art more in *England*, than when thou wert here.

95

> More unto Others; but not so to Me
> Of old acquainted with thy secret worth:
> What half-lost I endure for want of Thee
> The World will read in this mis-shapen *Birth*:

> Fair had my *Psyche* been, had she at first
> By thy kinde-censuring hand been dress'd and nurst.[14]

These stanzas were written after Beaumont had been ejected from Peterhouse in 1644, while Crashaw was abroad, and they obviously testify to a close personal and literary relationship. It is interesting that Beaumont should regard Gregory of Nazianzanus as the 'soul-attracting Pattern' by which Crashaw framed his devotion in verse—a suggestion which has not been acknowledged, let alone followed up, by Crashaw's critics. A detailed examination of Crashaw's possible interest in Gregory would be beyond the scope of this study, but it is worth pointing out in general terms the contribution a reading of Gregory might have made to the poetic outlined in the stanzas from *Psyche*. Laudian theology encouraged familiarity with the early Church Fathers in order to assert continuity with the pre-Reformation church, and Beaumont himself quoted from one of Gregory's poems on the title-page of *Psyche*, and wrote a poem entitled 'S. Gregorie Naziansen'.

Gregory of Nazianzanus is perhaps the least-known of the three Cappadocian Fathers (the other two being Basil the Great and Gregory of Nyssa). His life 'paralleled the decisive transitional period between the Roman and Byzantine empires. For a brief period during his lifetime Christians and Classicists stood on equal terms, each arguing their own case'. Gregory was equally famous as an orator and as a theologian, and the coexistence of these two demands constituted a persistent tension in his life. Le Clerc pointed this out in a rather superficial way: 'He is also full of Ornaments taken out of History, or Heathenish Fables; nay, he speaks sometimes of the lat/t/er, as the Pagan Philosophers did, without openly rejecting them'.[15] But, despite his feeling for pagan ornament, Gregory came to be considered a mainstay of classical Christian theology, an orthodoxy that would certainly have pleased Beaumont. Gregory's theological orations, for example, which belong to his episcopacy at Constantinople, completed Trinitarianism by the formal statement of the deity of the holy spirit. This doctrine was ratified by the Council of Constantinople in 381, and confirmed by a second council in 382. Beaumont applauded Gregory's achievement:

> Why, Gregorie without Division can
> Untie this knott, and in that Union

A Triad find & prove; no Net
By Sophistick cunning set
Can trap his feet.

Gregory's life and teaching thus exemplified the subordination of
eloquence to unblemished theological orthodoxy, while his friendship with Basil the Great could be read in terms of another of
Beaumont's preoccupations. Le Clerc gave considerable space to
this friendship, and Beaumont applied to it his own baroque
notion of interpenetration:

Now Basil loves,
And lives, & moves
In Gregorie;
And mutuall He
Loves Basil back again, & lives
By that Life away He gives.
Thus when two Floods imbrace, they loose each other
In the pellucid Bosome of his Brother.[16]

Again, he employs the imagery of flow to define the loss and restoration of selfhood, while the progressive expansion of line-length
enacts the movement towards a greater reciprocity.

In the fourth Canto of *Psyche*, Beaumont had criticised
Spenser's versification for being 'manacled in thick and peevish
Rhyme', and he himself preferred forms which were fluid rather
than patterned, inspiring in the reader not so much a sense of
stable order as an abandonment or outflow of self. Gregory may
have been an influence in this respect, although by his validation
of ecstatic eloquence rather than by his own verse. 'It may be
said of his *Poems*', Le Clerc wrote, 'that the Style of them is as
Prosaick, as that of his *Orations* is Elevated'. The orations develop
precisely that mode of 'cumulative ardor' which Warren considers characteristic of Crashaw's poetry. According to Le Clerc,
'*Gregory* doth seldom confine himself to one Subject only, and
observe an Order clear and free from Digressions'. His speeches
are:

1st. Without any great Order: Thoughts are heaped one upon
another, as they came into the Author's Mind; . . . *2dly.* His
Reasonings seem too far-fetch'd, and are not very convincing;

. . . 3*dly*. The Style of that *Oration* is too full of Figures, little correct, and even sometimes harsh; all which things often breed Obscurity. However, it must be confest, that he abounds in noble Comparisons, and happy and Energick Expressions.[17]

Gregory's orations, in short, fell foul of neo-classical taste for the same reasons that Crashaw's poetry did; they emphasised the loss of self in rapture rather than the controlling function of mind, the value of 'locutionary form' rather than of 'propositional content'.

Shelford's *Discourses* had defined charity as the noblest virtue: 'Faith converts the minde to God: but it is love and charitie that converts the heart and will to God, which is the greatest and last conversion, because we never seek anything untill we desire it'. This emphasis on virtue as affection was reinforced by their defini- tion of a third important term, devotion, which 'is the soul to prayer and the rest of Gods service, because it is a daughter of the mother-vertue Charitie: and this is a cheerfull and free giving of our selves to Gods service, as his houshold servants . . . And this devotion is derived *a voto, from a vow*, and is a frank gift and free binding of our selves unto it'. Shelford defined charity as desire— the soul's 'sanctified appetite', the heart's 'pulse to Godward'— and as a symbolic exchange, the free gift of the self in exchange for spiritual assurance. Its function was to 'bend and order' all the other virtues 'to Godward . . . For every action, as the learned know, proceeds from election; election is in the will, and the prin- cipal power of the will is love and charitie'. Hooker, too, had iden- tified the will with 'Choice', but he had devoted more attention to the antecedent cognitive decision as to what is or is not a worthy object of worship: 'Goodness is seen with the eye of the under- standing. And the light of that eye, is reason'.[18] Laudian theology concentrated not on the primary decision in favour of the good, but on the secondary willed election, the abandonment of self, and this emphasis—intensified by baroque notions of flow and inter- penetration—underlay Crashaw's poetry.

Crashaw's commendatory poem on the *Discourses* singled out Shelford's discussion of charity for praise; love became the major theme of his poetry, and he occasionally employed devotional method.[19] Indeed, one might note that the devotional writer St Francis de Sales, whose influence on Crashaw has been argued convincingly, understood the abandonment of self-love, rather than critical self-examination, to be the key to faith.[20] Crashaw was fascinated by the abandonment of self involved in mystical experience and in martyrdom. The 'Hymn to Sainte Teresa', for example, celebrates the rightness of the choice made by a six-year-old girl, a choice which cannot have been reasoned but rather impelled by a mysterious chárity:

> Yet though she cannot tell you why,
> She can LOVE, and she can DY.

Love impels the believer to a decision which is experienced as a movement from one level of being to another, the absorption of self-hood into communion thróugh participatory word and gesture. Crashaw's poems tend to focus on a liminal moment within this process of willed election, and his fascination with thresholds can be seen, for example, in the epigram 'Easter Day' which, as Williams notes, 'assembles the images of becoming: Heire, Tombe . . . the East (the dawn), the Nest, Morne, bud, and birth'.[21] All of these images focus on the point or state immediately prior to the emergence of á new order of being. Crashaw's own faith was by no means totally assured, and his conversion to Roman Catholicism was attended by all the difficulties of decision. Not surprisingly, he often explored the moment of decision—the threshold of new experience—and the two most telling examples of this concern are the exhortatory poems addressed to the Countess of Denbigh and to Mrs M. R. The 1652 *Sacred Poems* placed 'On a Prayer Booke Sent to Mrs. M. R.', together with 'To the same Party Councel', immediately after the Teresa poems. Both employ the characteristic parallel between secular and divine love, exhorting the recipient to pass from one level of being to another. Charity, Shelford wrote, 'is the lust and desire of the spirit, as concupiscence is the lust and desire of the flesh; the one sanctifieth and justifieth, the other damnifieth and condemneth . . . As concupiscence is the root of all vices; so this is the root of all vertues'.[22] Crashaw concentrated on the passage from concupiscence to charity, and on the decision that involved. The religious commitment of the Countess of Denbigh, whom he may have met first at Oxford in 1644, was notoriously unstable, and his poem to her focuses unerringly on the moment of decision:

> What heav'n-intreated HEART is This?
> Stands trembling at the gate of blisse;

> Holds fast the door, yet dares not venture
> Fairly to open it, and enter.
> Whose DEFINITION is a doubt
> Twixt life and death, twixt in and out.
> Say, lingering fair! why comes the birth
> Of your brave soul so slowly forth.
> Plead your pretences (o you strong
> In weaknes) why you choose so long
> In labor of your selfe to ly,
> Nor daring quite to live nor dy?[23]

The liminal moment involves a labour of self, an ambiguous state 'twixt in and out'. But Crashaw was concerned not with the moment itself, so much as with the possibility of conducting the uncertain believer through it into a different order of experience. He hoped to negotiate that passage by means of the transforming ceremonies of Catholicism and of poetry. Always sympathetic to Laudian practice, and himself developing a poetic based on the flowing transfusing power of form, Crashaw encountered Cowley as a man convinced of the validity of 'locutionary truth'.

III

'On Hope, By Way of Question and Answere, between A. Cowley and R. Crashawe', probably written while both men were at Cambridge, was first published in *Steps to the Temple* (1646). Cowley's contribution appeared, slightly altered, in *The Mistress*, together with his own defence of hope.[24] Nathanael Culverwel, in a treatise on religious assurance, introduced a distinction which is precisely that between the attitudes expressed by Cowley and Crashaw in 'On Hope':

> There's a vast difference between the Moralists hope, and that which is the Theological grace, and yet this is scarce took notice of; they require these three ingredients into the object of hope: that it must be (1) *bonum*, (2) *futurum*, (3) *incertum*; but Christian hope is certain & infallible, it looks upon good as to come, and as certain to come . . . Christian hope is nothing but a waiting and expectation of a certain good.

The real issue is the certainty or uncertainty of hope. If ones ends are of this world, then hope is an ambiguous virtue, a psychological aberration which may impair ones perception of reality, and thus prevent one from achieving those ends. If, however, ones ends are not of this world, a virtue which, by positing an alternative set of values, enables one to move onto another level of being can only be regarded as 'certain & infallible'. Hope, according to this scheme, initiates the abandonment of self-love which enables the believer to transcend the play of chance and necessity. It guides him through the liminal moment separating worldliness from faith and must therefore be regarded, not as a psychological aberration, but as an infallible mentor: 'Christian hope when 'tis in full vigour, is all one with assurance'.[25] The optimism engendered by the theological definition of hope can be seen, as Bertonasco points out, in the emphasis of the devotional method of St Francis de Sales and in Crashaw's poetry; it contrasts strongly with the scepticism of the secular definition. The genuine believer, St Paul had written, is characterised by a 'rejoicing in hope' (Romans 12, 12).

Cowley's argument against hope is thoroughly sceptical, very much in the manner of Culverwel's Moralists, although never properly scholastic. Already, at the time of *The Mistress* (which of course included 'Against Hope'), he seems to be curiously 'ahead of himself'; his analysis of hope, attempting statements with a high 'propositional content', sits uneasily beside the effort of many poems in the collection to operate a traditional code. Unlike love, hope was a psychological state to be narrowly plotted and defined rather than appealed to or inveighed against:

> Hope, whose weake being ruin'd is
> Alike, if it succeed, and if it misse.
> Whom Ill, and Good doth equally confound,
> And both the hornes of Fates dilemma wound.
>> Vaine shadow! that doth vanish quite
>> Both at full noone, and perfect night.
>> The Fates have not a possibility
>>> Of blessing thee.
> If things then from their ends wee happy call,
> 'Tis hope is the most hopelesse thing of all.[26]

Hope is 'weake' because 'ruin'd' by success and failure alike.

Faced by the 'double madnes' of equally damaging alternatives, it can only result in pain and bewilderment, and Cowley's definition, although deft and witty, is not without bluntness: 'The Fates have not a possibility/Of blessing thee'. Metrically, the stanza narrows down to the exact force of this statement, a concision bordering on harshness. Confronted by inescapable paradox, Cowley, like the lover in *The Mistress*, can only coin further paradoxes: ' 'Tis hope is the most hopelesse thing of all'. His next two stanzas explore both horns of fate's dilemma: the way in which hope preempts the pleasure of success, and its inability to guard against the misery of failure. The imagery of these stanzas constitutes a sequence of fine distinctions, as if Cowley were focusing a microscope, substituting one lens for another. Except that the revelatory moment of perfect focus never arrives; hope eludes definition, appearing and disappearing in the slide of one image over another. As with several poems in *The Mistress*, the technique of apostrophe mark the poet's entrapment in paradox. For hope, Cowley concludes, is a child of 'fond desire',

> That blows the Chymicks, and the Lovers fire,
>   Still leading them insensibly on,
>   With the strange witchcraft of *Anon*.
> By thee the one doth changing Nature through
>   Her endlesse Laborinths pursue,
> And th'other chases woman, while she goes
> More wayes, and turnes, then hunted Nature knowes.

Like alchemy and desire, hope involves the endless postponing of fulfilment, the 'strange witchcraft of *Anon*'. It intervenes in the normal working of the mind and operates along the axis of temporal succession, denying and denied possession of the object of desire. This stanza has none of the painful concision of stanza 1, as if metre itself had been stretched and frustrated by the sluggish process of deferment.

Theological hope, on the other hand, operates along the vertical axis of experience, as the *rite de passage* between one level of being to another. St Paul represented God as 'he who has begotten us again to a living hope', by sacrificing his son (I Peter 1, 3). This hope should be regarded as the passage from one level to another, a condition between the 'no longer' and the 'not yet', 'forgetting those things which are behind, and reaching forth unto those things which are before' (Philippians 3, 13). Crashaw himself, in his 'Hymn to the Name of Jesus', recognised hope as a type of assurance which operates within the liminal moment:

> O see, The WEARY liddes of wakefull Hope
> (LOVE's Eastern windowes) All wide ope
> With Curtains drawn,
> To catch The Day-break of Thy DAWN.[27]

Hope, sometimes figured during the seventeenth century as an anchor cast up to heaven,[28] is the link and passage between human uncertainty and the state of assured grace. It guarantees ontological continuity, which Paul terms the resurrection of the *soma*: faith, hope, and love abide in the consummation (I Corinthians 13, 13). Crashaw's reply to Cowley follows the theological definition of hope:

> Sweet *Hope*! kind cheat! faire fallacy! by thee
> Wee are not where, or what wee bee,
> But what, and where wee would bee: thus art thou
> Our absent presence, and our future now.

Hope is a valid and beneficial fallacy not because it deludes man, but because it substitutes a divine for a secular frame of reference, a higher reality for a lower. It is certainly paradoxical, an 'absent presence' and 'future now', but these paradoxes are designed to prepare the believer for a radically different order of experience rather than, as Cowley thought, to bewilder and entrap him.

In order to prove his case rhetorically, Crashaw did not so much answer Cowley's argument on its own terms as introduce a new frame of reference altogether. He had to find a language which would assimilate and transform the implicit secular assumptions of Cowley's definition, and he did this by a *ceremonial* reordering of Cowley's 'propositional' images. Each image in Cowley's argument is a discrete unit of measurement designed to locate and hold a particular meaning; the images do not add up to anything because hope is a conceptual mirage. Stanza, metre, and rhyme simply marshal those units into an effective statement. Crashaw, on the other hand, picks up an image from Cowley—

> For joy, like Wine kept close, doth better taste:
> If it take ayre before, its spirits waste

—and, by incorporating it into a continuum, transforms it:

> Faire *Hope*! our earlier Heaven! by thee
> Young *Time* is taster to Eternity.
> Thy generous wine with age growes strong, not sower;
> Nor need wee kill thy fruit to smell thy flower.
>   Thy golden head never hangs downe,
>   Till in the lap of Loves full noone
>   It falls, and dyes: oh no, it melts away
>   As doth the dawne into the day:
> As lumpes of sugar lose themselves, and twine
> Their subtile essence with the soule of Wine.

The image is not merely turned back against Cowley, but rather fitted into the movement of a ceremonial utterance which remoulds and extends it, drawing out in the last two lines implications which it never had for Cowley. Crashaw has thus demonstrated by his use of imagery the access of new meaning which faith brings, and this access is very much a function of the power of ceremonial utterance, of the 'person propounding' rather than of the 'proposition itself'. For example, lines 5–8 of the stanza I have just quoted owe some of their strength and balance to a previous rehearsal of the image in 'Charitas Nimia'.[29] The interjection 'oh no', although without semantic content, contributes to the meaning of the stanza by performing uplift—the gradual raising of personal commitment from hope to faith by such virtually imperceptible stages as the transition from 'It falls, and dyes' to 'it melts away'. The voicing of truth is the only possible form of definition and argument. The poem itself becomes a Pauline 'rejoicing in hope', a ceremony, and its conclusion fuses, by a witty transposition, the orders of nature and grace:

> Though the vext Chymick chases
> His fugitive gold through all her faces,
> And loves more fierce, more fruitlesse fires assay
>   One face more fugitive then all they,
> True *Hope's* a glorious Huntresse, and her chase
> The God of Nature in the field of Grace.

Cowley's concluding stanza arranges the images of alchemy and of secular passion in parallel, without any development from one to the other. Crashaw, however, places the two images in an ascending order, maintaining continuity by his use of a metallurgical term (assay), but introducing a comparative: 'more fugitive' for 'fugitive'. He is, as ever, concerned to initiate a movement from one level of experience to another, a *rite de passage*, whereas Cowley's argument develops on one level only, attributing equal meaning (or lack of meaning) to all phenomena. My treatment of 'On Hope' has inevitably failed to do justice to the complex interaction of tone and intensity between the two arguments, but I hope I have demonstrated that two radically different cultural attitudes, rather than simply two dissimilar temperaments, confront each other in the poem. The order of ceremony and of spoken truth sustains Crashaw's theological definition of hope, enabling him to regard it as a crucial moment in the crossing between levels which produces an abandonment of self, or a symbolic exchange of selfhood for communion. Cowley, on the other hand, can only understand hope as a 'double madnes' which reveals the weakness of the self when confronted by a paradox it can neither avoid nor resolve. Hope, like desire, persecutes the self with its 'strange witchcraft of *Anon*', condemning man to temporality and flux.

One might gather, from 'Upon two greene Apricockes' and from Cowley's elegy, that Crashaw, the elder man, had been cast in the role of teacher, or even of father-figure, but one ought not to imagine that Crashaw learnt nothing from Cowley; if this were so, their relationship would not have the dimension it does. For example, Cowley did, I believe, influence Crashaw's reformulation of the 'Letter to the Countess of Denbigh'. Crashaw left the first version of the 'Letter' with Carre in Paris when he went to Italy in 1646, and it was included in *Carmen Deo Nostro* (1652). The second version, written without consultation with Carre, was published as a separate pamphlet in London in 1653, and the two versions differ considerably in their technique of argument. Both are religious persuasions cast as love poems, but the first keeps to the limits of Crashaw's devotional vocabulary, while the second develops a more diffuse method of argument by imagery. The characteristic devotional intensity of the following lines in the first version—

> Meet his well-meaning Wounds, wise heart!
> And hast to drink the wholesome dart.
> That healing shaft, which heavn till now

> Hath in love's quiver hid for you.
> O Dart of love! arrow of light!
> O happy you, if it hitt right,
> It must not fall in vain, it must
> Not mark the dry regardless dust.
> Fair one, it is your fate; and brings
> Aeternall worlds upon it's wings.
> Meet it with wide-spread armes; and see
> It's seat your soul's just center be

—was superseded by a witty and extended imagistic argument. Crashaw even employed the scholastic thesis that heavy objects demonstrate their love of God by falling. According to Anthony Wood, when Crashaw was in Paris, 'being a meer Scholar and very shiftless, Mr. Abr. Cowley the Poet, did, upon intimation of his being there, find him out in a sorry condition, an. 1646 or thereabouts'. Cowley was at that time writing *The Mistress*, and deploying precisely the sort of witty, rather abstract imagery which Crashaw imported into the second version of the 'Letter'. These lines, added to the second version—

> Both Winds and Waters urge their way,
> And murmure if they meet a stay,
> Mark how the curl'd Waves work and wind,
> All hating to be left behind.
> Each bigge with businesse thrusts the other,
> And seems to say, Make haste, my Brother[30]

—seem to echo Cowley's 'Bathing in the River':

> The amo'rous *Waves* would fain about her stay,
> But still new am'orous *waves* drive them away,
> And with swift current to those joys they haste,
> That do as swiftly waste . . .   (P, 150)

Crashaw even uses a virtually identical rhyme-pair (way/stay), and it must have been he who imitated Cowley, rather than the other way round, because the second version of the 'Letter' was written after he had left Paris. This would not have been the first time Crashaw had used erotic imagery to encourage a 'pulse to Godward'; 'On a Prayer Booke' alludes to the most notorious of seventeenth-century erotic poems, Carew's 'Rapture'.[31] It seems natural that Crashaw should have paid some attention to what his friend was doing, and the reformulation of the 'Letter' seems to me evidence of his respect for Cowley's poetry.

IV

The history of this encounter between radically different personalities and cultural assumptions provides a context for the generosity of Cowley's elegy 'On the Death of Mr. Crashaw', the last poem in the *Miscellanies*:

> *Poet* and *Saint*! to thee alone are given
> The two most sacred *Names* of *Earth* and *Heaven*.
> The hard and rarest *Union* which can be
> Next that of *Godhead* with *Humanitie*. (P, 48)

By undergoing a double ceremony, a double baptism, Crashaw has opened the vertical relation between God and man, slipped through the *rite de passage*, and thus singled himself out from the throng of profane poets:

> Ah wretched *We, Poets of Earth*! but *Thou*
> Wert *Living* the same *Poet* which thou'rt *Now*.
> Whilst *Angels* sing to thee their ayres divine,
> And joy in an applause so great as *thine*.
> Equal society with them to hold,
> Thou need'st not make *new Songs*, but say the *Old*.
> And they (kind Spirits!) shall all rejoyce to see
> How little less then *They, Exalted Man* may be.

But whereas Crashaw's old songs had constituted an act of self-transcendence, an optimistic bracketing of the worldly frame of reference, Cowley has no such assurance, particularly when contemplating the state of poetry:

> Still the old *Heathen Gods* in *Numbers* dwell,
> The *Heav'enliest* thing on Earth still keeps up *Hell*.

> Nor have we yet quite purg'd the *Christian Land*;
> Still *Idols* here, like *Calves* at *Bethel* stand.
> And though *Pans Death* long since all *Oracles* broke,
> Yet still in Rhyme the *Fiend Apollo* spoke:
> Nay with the worst of Heathen dotage We
> (Vain men!) the *Monster Woman Deifie*;
> Find *Stars*, and tye our *Fates* there in a *Face*,
> And *Paradise* in them by whom we *lost* it, place.

Secular love-poetry represents a *false* ceremony, not a symbolic exchange of selfhood for 'equal society' with angels, but a 'dotage', an enslavement to desire and illusion. The weak parenthesis 'Vain men!', when the suspension of the previous line has led one to expect an emphatic verb, neatly emphasises Cowley's despair at the single dimension of modern concerns, and their inability to move, as Crashaw had done by proper ceremony, from one level to another. He himself, the author of *The Mistress*, is forced to recognise both the value of Crashaw's saintliness and the reality of his own situation among the '*Idols* here'. While he can celebrate the former, he must also reflect on the latter, and is thus forced to bring two different rhetorics into play. His eloquence can follow the events of Crashaw's life, reinventing the code according to which it was lived (the terms, the images, the sacred places), or it can turn back on his own observance of weaker—sometimes false—codes, his relative homelessness:

> Pardon, my *Mother Church*, if I consent
> That *Angels* led him when from thee he went,
> For even in *Error* sure no *Danger* is
> When joyn'd with so much *Piety* as *His*.
> Ah, mighty *God*, with shame I speak't, and grief,
> Ah that our greatest *Faults* were in *Belief*!
> And our weak *Reason* were ev'en weaker yet,
> Rather then thus our *Wills* too strong for it.
> His *Faith* perhaps in some nice Tenents might
> Be wrong; his *Life*, I'm sure, was *in the right*.
> And I my self a *Catholick* will be,
> So far at least, great *Saint*, to *Pray* to thee.

He comments here on his own statement in the preceding couplet that angels had borne Crashaw in triumph to Loretto, and so away from the Anglican Church. That statement had been a consciously ceremonial utterance, a reinvention of the code which sustained Crashaw's faith; but the code it reinvented was not one that Cowley, an orthodox Anglican, could credit. This paragraph therefore tries to explain to the reader why he has made a statement which strictly speaking has no 'propositional truth'. He consented to the factual error, he says, because it was more important to celebrate the intensity and durability of Crashaw's faith than to question its nature; the criterion of 'locutionary truth' overrides the criterion of 'propositional truth'. The strength and subtlety of the poem derive from its willingness to acknowledge the claims of both criteria, to celebrate but also to analyse its own mode of celebration. (One thinks of Marvell's 'On Paradise Lost', not so much a formal encomium as an account of his own developing response to Milton's epic. Indeed, the turn of that poem—'Pardon me, mighty poet . . .'—perhaps owes something to the turn of Cowley's elegy—'Pardon, my *Mother Church* . . .'.)

Cowley's problem then was how finally to reconcile the two criteria: 'locutionary' and 'propositional', ceremonial and private. How could he reassert the tone of ceremonial lament without sacrificing his awareness of the complexities of this particular friendship? He did so by employing the conceit of the ascent of Elijah, which was an overtly ceremonial device,[32] but also encompassed an intimate personal relationship:

> Thou from low earth in nobler *Flames* didst rise,
> And like *Elijah*, mount *Alive* the skies.
> *Elisha*-like (but with a wish much less,
> More fit thy *Greatness*, and my *Littleness*)
> Lo here I beg (I whom thou once didst prove
> So humble to *Esteem*, so Good to *Love*)
> Not that thy *Spirit* might on me *Doubled* be,
> I ask but *Half* thy mighty *Spirit* for Me.
> And when my *Muse* soars with so strong a Wing,
> 'Twill learn of things *Divine*, and first of *Thee* to sing.

The parentheses work to qualify the conceit and to anchor it in the lived experience of a particular relationship. Cowley identifies Crashaw unambiguously with a ceremonial role, that of the prophet-saint moving 'in nobler *Flames*' from the level of this world to the level of the next. He himself is both inside this ceremony (as

'Elisha'), and outside, commenting on it parenthetically in the light of the truth of their friendship. The poem reproduces, in its switching of rhetorics and unevenness of tone, the conflict between criteria of truth; it makes out of that conflict a just and forceful elegy.

5 The Sacred Poem

I

Cowley's resolve, formulated in the elegy on Crashaw, to write about 'things *Dvine*' found expression in his epic poem about the life of David, the *Davideis*. In his *Life* of Cowley, Thomas Sprat made out that the poem had been 'wholly written' early in Cowley's career, before the outbreak of civil war, but I think we should place it in the period between 1650 and 1654, as Kermode has argued.[1] I shall show that the *Davideis* expresses anti-monarchist sentiments quite explicit enough to trouble Sprat, who was only too aware of the harm further revelations about Cowley's wavering political loyalties might do. Sprat could not, perhaps, suppress parts of the poem, in the way he had suppressed a part of the 1656 Preface, but he could reduce the chances of people scouring it for political allusions by claiming that it was 'wholly written' *before* the Great Rebellion—by dissociating it from the early 1650s, the period of Cowley's return to England and acquiescence in Republican rule. The *Davideis* was not, like *The Mistress*, an apprenticeship, the occupation of an already privileged form; rather, it attempted to revive and to alter a traditional code (epic convention) in such a way as to produce a new message (the Word of God):

> Too long the *Muses-Land* have *Heathen* bin;
> Their *Gods* too long were *Dev'ils*, and *Vertues Sin*;
> But *Thou, Eternal Word*, hast call'd forth *Me*
> Th'*Apostle*, to convert that *World* to *Thee*;
> T'unbind the charms that in slight *Fables* lie,
> And teach that *Truth* is *truest Poesie*. (P, 243)

The ambiguity I have already noted in the 1656 Preface persists here: on one hand, the new poetic will replace fabling by real knowledge; but this real knowledge, on the other hand, will be transmitted in accordance with the same criterion of truth, our faith in the 'person propounding' ('Th' *Apostle*, to convert that *World* to *Thee*'). It seems furthermore, to judge by the intensity of Cowley's tone, that he has arrived at a crossroads, at the moment of his calling to a difficult but supremely important task; the mantle worn by Crashaw-Elijah has fallen on his shoulders. Any ambiguity in his conception of the task assigned to poetry was bound to be magnified by the scale of his project.

Indeed, the ambiguity became so blatant he decided to abandon the poem after four books. *The Civil War* had proved impossible to write, partly because history came up with the wrong plot, partly because it was in any case already at odds with itself. In the *Davideis*, too, we witness the failure of a form to contain and synthesise disparate rhetorics, and the two poems should certainly be read in relation. Although not a record of contemporary events the epic is, in part at least, political, caught in the violent swirl of allegiances produced by civil war. Over forty years ago Nethercot, in his biography of Cowley, argued that Book IV of the *Davideis* was designed as a political allegory, an argument which has since been neither confirmed nor denied, indeed barely discussed at all.[2] In Book IV, David describes to Moab the origins of the Jewish monarchy, and the characters of Saul and Jonathan, material which, in seventeenth-century eyes, was certainly capable of allegorical interpretation. As William Creed put it, in a sermon preached on 28 June 1660: 'The Author of this book of *Samuel*, or the *Kings*, seemes to have been a Register of our times, and to have foretold of these same changes, we in our days have lived to see'.[3] The Argument to Book IV, with its references to 'the Change of Government in Israel', and 'the Motives for which the people desired a King', indicates clearly enough that it may be read as a political statement, but gives no clue to the kind of statement it might be. Similarly, David's speech to Moab is, as Nethercot remarks, 'replete' with references to improper government and to conflict, but again Cowley gives no specific indication as to how they should be interpreted. Nethercot, however, insists that the Book should be read as a specific allegory of the state of the nation: 'Most significant of all . . . was the extended discussion of the advisability of surrendering the commonwealth form of government under the Judges for a revived monarchy—the same question that was agitating all England at the time' (i.e. during the early 1650s). But it seems to me unlikely that Cowley ever considered Cromwell's regime in any way equivalent to the rule of the Judges over Israel. 'Commonwealth', in his usage, is a neutral term and not related to any particular historical regime. Finally, the monarchy instituted by Samuel was in no sense a 'revived monarchy', nor does Cowley describe it as such. Nethercot reads his own preoccupations not only into the use of a term like 'commonwealth', but also into the Bible itself, and it is surely unwise to suggest that the figure of Samuel in the *Davideis* is a 'flattering' representation of Cromwell. Samuel is noble and strong, but also regarded as a '*Dotard*' by his people; there were certainly more plausible representations available, even in the same biblical episode.[4] Similarly, Nethercot discerns 'unmistakeable references to the attempts of Charles II against the Commonwealth and to the weak characters of Cromwell's sons', but the assertion seems to me unwarranted. If Book IV is allegorical, it is a vague and partial allegory, and one that Cowley's contemporaries do not seem to have noticed at all.

Nethercot's argument, although I think mistaken, does at least serve to draw attention to the political content of the Book. But that content must be understood not as a political allegory, but as a political statement: a statement about the nature of power and authority, and particularly about the consequences of the abuse of power. Moab's initial request to David invites such a statement:

> And pray, kind *Guest*, whilst we ride thus (says he)
> (To gameful *Nebo* still three leagues there be)
> The story of your *royal friend* relate;
> And his ungovern'd *Sires* imperious fate,
> Why your great State that nameless Fam'ily chose,
> And by what steps to *Israels Throne* they rose.   (P, 366)

Moab is interested in Saul the 'ungovern'd' tyrant, and the ambiguity of the term 'imperious'—at what point does the prerogative of authority become arrogance or abuse?—sets the tone of David's reply. The fact that Saul's family was 'nameless', and that he therefore did not inherit power, means that the way is open for a discussion of the basis of monarchy *per se*. David starts by discussing the four hundred years between Joshua and Saul, a period which has no possible place in Nethercot's allegorical scheme, but which does bear very pertinently on the use and abuse of authority. This was a period of anarchy and, as Cowley remarks in a footnote, 'all the wickednesses and disorders that we read of during the time of the Judges, are attributed in Scripture to the want of a *King*' (note 9, P, 395). Authority was then constituted not by the apparatus of public office, but by divine calling:

> Oft pity'ing *God* did well-form'd *Spirits* raise,
> Fit for the toilsome business of their days,
> To free the groaning *Nation*, and to give
> *Peace* first, and then the *Rules* in *Peace* to live.
> But they whose stamp of *Power* did chiefly ly
> In *Characters* too fine for most mens *Ey*,
> *Graces* and *Gifts Divine*; not painted bright
> With state to awe *dull* minds, and force t'*affright*,
> Were ill obey'd whil'st *Living*, and at *death*,
> Their *Rules* and *Pattern* vanisht with their breath.
> The *hungry Rich* all near them did devour,
> Their *Judge* was *Appetite*, and their *Law* was *Power*.
>
> (P, 366–7)

It is a situation rather like that described by Denham at the end of the revised version of *Coopers Hill*, and Cowley acknowledges the urgency of a solution by his placement of a line-ending: '. . . and to give/*Peace* first . . .'. But authority has a double 'stamp of *Power*', internal and external, and the Israelites regard only the latter:

> They saw not *Powers* true *Source*, and scorn'd t'obey
> Persons that *look'd* no *dreadfuller* than *They*. (P, 369)

The real question, then, a question of enormous importance to Cowley's contemporaries, was how far monarchy—so far mentioned only as a lack, in a footnote—represented a 'true *Source*' of power. Could the internal and external marks of political authority be reconciled in the person of a king? According to Cowley, the example of Saul proves otherwise:

> Yet was he wise all dangers to foresee;
> But born t'*affright*, and not to *fear* was *He*.
> His *Wit* was *strong*; not *Fine*; and on his tongue

An *Artless grace* above all *Eloq'uence* hung.
These *Virtues* too the rich unusual dress
Of *Modesty* adorn'd and *Humbleness.*
Like a clear *Varnish* o're fair *Pictures* laid,
More *fresh* and *Lasting* they the *Colours* made.
Till *Power* and *violent Fortune,* which did find
No stop or bound, o'rewhelm'd no less his *Mind,*
Did, *Deluge-like,* the nat'ural forms deface,
And brought forth unknown *Monsters* in their place.

(P, 374)

Again, the image of a violently destructive deluge recalls Denham, and this swamping of rationality is underlined by the only enjambement in the passage:

Till *Power* and *violent Fortune,* which did find
No stop or bound, o'rewhelm'd no less his Mind . . .

David's account of the rule of the Judges, from Joshua to Samuel, opens the question of the 'stamp of *Power*' and the '*Characters*' which inscribe it on the person of the ruler; it poses this question largely in terms of the relationship between internal and external sources of authority. These matters were obviously of immediate political relevance, as were the terms of Cowley's discussion. John Cleveland, for example, described the rightful monarch as 'carrying Gods stamp and mark among men'.[5] But Cowley was concerned not so much to support the claims of any specific leader, as to examine in a more abstract way the function, or malfunction, of political authority. He saw the period between Joshua and Samuel as an uncontrolled oscillation between the violence of anarchy and the violence of tyranny. Did the institution of monarchy, then, provide a 'stop or bound' to this dangerous alternation of evils? Did it reconcile internal and external authority so as to provide a form of government that was both just and effective? Because of the misconduct of Samuel's sons, there were 'just and faultless causes' why the 'general voice' should cry out for monarchy (P, 369). God, however,

ill grains did in this *Incense* smell,
Wrapt in fair *Leaves* he saw the *Canker* dwell.
A mut'inous Itch of *Change,* a dull *Despair*

> Of helps *divine*, oft prov'd; a faithless care
> Of *Common Means*; the pride of heart, and scorn
> Of th'*humble yoke* under low *Judges* born.
> They saw the state and glittering pomp which blest
> In vulgar sense the *Scepters* of the *East*.   (P, 369)

Original sin—'pride of heart'—reasserts itself in this demand for a king. Monarchy is a human institution and therefore a matter of external authority only, of the 'state and glittering pomp' which impresses 'vulgar sense'.

Cowley drives this point home by his polemical version of Samuel's speech to the Israelites (I Samuel 8) on the nature and prerogative of monarchy, a speech which was probably the most controversial of all the biblical texts cited in the bitter seventeenth-century debates about the proper form of government. It had, for example, been widely used by the proponents of absolute monarchy, who argued that Samuel was warning the people of their complete subjection to the will of the monarch, against which there could be no redress. James I took the 'grounde' of the 'dutie and allegeance, that the Lieges owe to their King', out of 'the wordes of SAMUEL, dited by Gods spirit, when God had given him commandment to heare the peoples voyce in choosing and anoynting them a King. And because that place of Scripture being well understood is pertinent for our purpose, I have inserte herein the very words of the text'. He then quoted I Samuel 8, 9–20 and concluded that it was meant to prepare the Israelites 'to the due obedience of that King, which God was to give unto them'. Most important of all, the text stated that under no circumstances could the 'Lieges' resist the will of their monarch: 'And therfore in time arme your selves with patience & humility, since he, that hath the only power to un make him; & ye only to obey, bearing with these straits that I now fore shew you, as with the finger of God, which lyeth not in you to take off'. Charles I, had he recognised the High Court of Justice, would apparently have employed the same argument from Scripture in his own defence. 'It seems', John Cook wrote,

> that one passage which the King would have offered to the court . . . was that I Sam. 8 is a copy of the King's commission, by vertue whereof he, as King, might rule and govern as he list, that he might take the peoples sons and appoint them for

himself for his chariots, and to be his horsemen, and to take their daughters to be his confectionaries, and take their fields and vineyards and olive yards even the best of them and their goodliest young men and their asses, and give them to his officers and servants. Which, indeed, is a copy and patern of an absolute tyrant and absolute slaves, where the people have no more then the tyrant will afford them. The Holy Spirit in that chapter does not insinuate what a good King ought to be, but what a wicked King would presume to do.

Cook conveniently summarises the alternative interpretations—absolutist and republican—of Samuel's speech. But Charles's case was also made for him by Robert Filmer, an equally uncompromising, although not necessarily influential, political theorist. In his *Patriarcha*, probably written before 1640, Filmer argued that:

> the scope of Samuel was to teach the people a dutiful obedience to their King, even in those things which themselves did esteem mischievous and inconvenient. For, by telling them what a King would do, he instructs them what a subject must suffer. Yet not so that it is right for Kings to do injury, but it is right for them to go unpunished by the people if they do it. So that in this point it is all one whether Samuel describe a King or a tyrant for patient obedience is due to both. No remedy in the text against tyrants, but in crying and praying unto God in that day.

'This', Hobbes commented on the import of the speech, 'is absolute power, and summed up in the last words, *you shall be his servants*'.[6] All these writers assume, in Cook's words, that I Samuel 8 concerns 'what a good King ought to be' and not 'what a wicked King would presume to do'.

Their political opponents, on the other hand, thought that Samuel was warning the Israelites of the dire consequences of monarchy, and that the people were therefore mistaken in their choice. Cowley compared the desire of the Jews for a king to the slavish reverence for external marks of authority found in Eastern countries—

> They saw the state and glittering pomp which blest
> In vulgar sense the *Scepters* of the *East*

—and Milton made the same point in *The Tenure of Kings and Magistrates*: 'Although generally the people of Asia, and with them the Jews also, especially since the time they chose a King against the advice and counsel of God, are noted by wise Authors as much inclinable to slavery'. In attributing slavishness to Eastern peoples, both men were following a tradition established by Aristotle, and developed by Bodin and Calvin. At any rate, when Cowley came to write his version of Samuel's speech, he added a footnote which places his interpretation politically:

> It is a vile opinion of those men, and might be punished without *Tyranny*, if they teach it, who hold, that the *right* of *Kings* is set down by *Samuel* in this place. Neither did the people of *Israel* ever allow, or the *Kings* avow the assumption of such a power, as appears by the story of *Ahab* and *Naboth*. Some indeed did exercise it, but that is no more a proof of the *Right*, then their *Practise* was of the *Lawfulness* of *Idolatry*.   (Note 16, P, 396)

Cowley criticises the absolutist interpretation in the strongest terms, and he has certainly come a long way from the uncritical royalism of *The Civil War*, with its condemnation of Puritans who 'fling/All Texts of wicked *Princes* at their King' (II, 597). He agrees, in effect, with Cook's argument that Samuel is describing 'what a wicked King would presume to do', and the rhetorical slant of the speech itself bears this out:

> He bow'd, and ended here; and *Samuel* streight,
> Pawsing a while at this great questions weight,
> With a grave sigh, and with a thoughtful Ey
> That more of *Care* than *Passion* did descry,
> Calmly replys: You're sure the first (said he)
> Of *freeborn* men that begg'd for *Slavery*.
> I fear, my friends, with heav'enly *Manna* fed,
> (Our old forefathers crime) we lust for *Bread*.
> Long since by God from *Bondage* drawn, I fear,
> We build anew th' *Egyptian Brickiln* here.
> Cheat not your selves with *words*: for though a *King*
> Be the mild Name, a *Tyrant* is the *Thing*.   (P, 371).

And so on. Cowley's version is considerably more vehement than the biblical text, as for example when he transforms I Samuel 8, 13 ('And he will take your daughters to be confectionaries, and to be cooks, and to be bakers') into:

> Your *Daughters* and *dear Wives* he'll force away,
> His *Lux'ury* some, and some his *Lust* t'obey.

He loses few opportunities to reinforce or to supplement anything in the original which might be construed as a warning against monarchy, and his overall tone comes surprisingly close to that of Milton, whose definition of a tyrant in *The Tenure of Kings* was equally uncompromising:

> And because his power is great, his will boundless and exorbitant, the fulfilling whereof is for the most part accompanied with innumerable wrongs and oppressions of the people, murders massachers, rapes, adulteries, desolation, and subversion of Citties and whole Provinces, look how great a good and happiness a just King is, so great a mischeife is a Tyrant; as hee the public father of his Countrie, so this the common enemie. Against whom what the people lawfully may doe, as against a common pest, and destroyer of mankinde, I suppose no man of cleare judgement need goe furder to be guided then by the very principles of nature in him.

Milton, however, backs up this attack on the abuse of power with a vindication of democratic rights:

> It follows lastly, that since the King or Magistrate holds his authoritie of the people, both originaly and naturally for their good in the first place, and not his own, then may the people as oft as they shall judge it for the best, either choose him or reject him, retaine him or depose him though no Tyrant, meerly by the liberty and right of free born Men, to be govern'd as seems to them best.[7]

According to his doctrine of popular sovereignty, the people may elect or depose rulers as they wish, and that is why Samuel did not deny their request for a king. Cowley, on the other hand, has reservations about the 'liberty and right of free born Men, to be govern'd as seems to them best', as is shown by Moab's response to David's rendering of I Samuel 8:

> Methinks (thus *Moab* interrupts him here)
> The good old *Seer* 'gainst *Kings* was too severe.
> 'Tis *Jest* to tell a *People* that they're *Free*,
> *Who*, or *How many* shall their *Masters* be
> Is the sole doubt; *Laws guid*, but cannot *reign*;
> And though they *bind* not Kings, yet they *restrain*. (P, 372)

Moab seems to be hinting at some kind of mixed or tempered monarchy, a balance of forces which would restrain without binding. David tries to deflect, rather than to answer, this counter-charge:

> 'Tis true, Sir, he replies;
> Yet men whom age and action renders wise,
> So much great changes fear, that they believe
> All evils *will*, which *may* from them arrive.   (P, 372)

In effect, he reiterates Cook's interpretation of Samuel's speech as a warning against 'what a wicked King would presume to do'. So the argument, which Cowley's footnote had designated as polemic, peters out, leaving only the rhetorical intensity of the speech itself. Kings are by definition tyrants—

> Cheat not your selves with *words*: for though a *King*
> Be the mild Name, a *Tyrant* is the *Thing*

—and the institution of monarchy will not, therefore, bring to an end the dangerous oscillation between anarchy and tyranny.

But there is another possible context for Cowley's attitude to monarchy. Hobbes's attitude to the election of Saul to be king was, as Pocock notes, suspended between 'emphasis that it constituted a 'rejection' and 'deposition' of God from his direct kingship over Israel, and insistence that this nevertheless occurred with his permission and consent, so that the authority of the kings was not merely natural, but had his express and positive sanction'.[8] Cowley's position was much closer to the first emphasis than to the second, as God's acceptance of the principle of monarchy, in a speech to Samuel, demonstrates:

> This stubborn Land sins still, nor is it *Thee*, but *Us*
> (Who have been so long their *King*) they seek to cast off thus.

Five hundred rolling years hath this stiff Nation strove
To 'exhaust the boundless stores of our unfathom'd *Love*.
Be't so then; yet once more are we resolv'd to try
T'outweary them through all their *Sins Variety*.
Assemble ten days hence the num'erous people here;
To draw the *Royal Lot* which our hid *Mark* shall bear.
Dismiss them now,in peace; but their next crime shall bring
Ruine without redress on *Them*, and on their *King*.   (P, 373)

God's sanction is altogether less 'express and positive' than
Hobbes would have allowed, and the really important point is
made in the first couplet: '*Us*/(Who have been so long their *King*)
they seek to cast off thus'. According to both men, God ruled
directly, via His prophets, during the period between Joshua and
Samuel. But this, as Hobbes remarked, was a period of lawless-
ness:

After the death of Joshua, till the time of Saul, the time between
is noted frequently in the Book of *Judges*, *That there was in those
days no king in Israel*; and sometimes with this addition, that *every
man did that which was right in his own eyes*. By which is to be understood, that where it is said, *there was no king*, is meant, *there was no
sovereign power* in Israel. And so it was, if we consider the act and
exercise of such power. For after the death of Joshua and
Eleazer, *there arose another generation* (*Judges* ii. 10, 11) *that knew not
the Lord, nor the works which he had done for Israel, but did evil in the
sight of the Lord, and served Baalim*.

After Joshua's death, Cowley wrote, there were

> Almost four hundred years from him to *Saul*,
> In too much freedom past, or forreign thral;   (P, 366)

and added in a footnote: 'For all the wickednesses and disorders
that we read of during the time of the Judges, are attributed in
Scripture to the want of a *King*. *And in those days was no King in Israel*'
(P, 395). Cowley's account, from which I have quoted above
(P, 89), of the Israelites' slavish reverence for external authority,
and of the anarchy this produced, reiterates Hobbes's observation
that there was

amongst them a great part, and probably the greatest part, that no longer than they saw great miracles, or, what is equivalent to a miracle, great abilities, or great felicity in the enterprises of their governors, gave sufficient credit either to the fame of Moses or to the colloquies between God and the priests; they took occasion, as oft as their governors displeased them, by blaming sometimes the policy, sometimes the religion, to change the government or revolt from their obedience at their pleasure: and from thence proceeded from time to time the civil troubles, divisions, and calamities of the nation.

(I do not think that Cowley's reference to '*Civil War*', the 'frequent curse of our loose-govern'd *State*', is any more allegorical—as Nethercot would have it—than Hobbes's reference to 'civil troubles, divisions, and calamities of the nation'.) The institution of monarchy represented an absolute break with the form of government exercised, in God's name, by the Judges:

Again, when the sons of Samuel (I *Sam*. vii. 3) being constituted by their father judges in Bersebee, received bribes, and judged unjustly, the people of Israel refused any more to have God to be their king, in other manner than he was king of other people; and therefore cried out to Samuel, to choose them a king after the manner of the nations. So that justice failing, faith also failed; insomuch, as they deposed their God, from reigning over them.

Monarchy is a human institution, and the decision to elect a king 'after the manner of the nations' was thus a rebellion against God. In Hobbes's scheme, Christ's mission involved the re-establishment of direct rule by God, 'so that it were superfluous to say in our prayer, *Thy kingdom come*, unless it be meant of the restoration of that kingdom of God by Christ, which by revolt of the Israelites had been interrupted in the election of Saul'.[9] 'If', as Pocock points out, 'the sole purpose of Christ's mission is to restore the immediate civil rule of God over his peculiar people which ended with the election of Saul, it might also seem as if that event constituted a second fall of man, something which the whole process of redemption exists to undo'.[10] Hobbes, he continues, does not go to these lengths, 'since he wishes to maintain the legitimacy of

Davidic kingship over the peculiar people', but Cowley, less certain of the virtues of monarchy, accuses Saul of a second 'original sin'. When Saul performs a sacrifice that should have been left for Samuel to perform, Samuel reproves him severely:

> His foul *Ingratitude* to heav'en he chid,
> To pluck that *Fruit* which was alone *forbid*
> To Kingly power in all that plenteous land,
> Where all things else submit to his command.
> And as fair *Edens* violated *Tree*,
> To'*Immortal Man* brought in *Mortalitie*:
> So shall that *Crown*, which God eternal meant,
> From thee (said he) and thy great house be rent,
> Thy Crime shall *Death* to all thine *Honours* send,
> And give thy'*Immortal Royalty* an *End*. (P, 384)

The final rhyme underscores the grim conclusion. In his feeling that monarchy represents a political reenactment of the Fall, Cowley seems to be close to another tradition of thought, based on Isaiah's prophecy that a return to rule by Judges would indicate the beginning of the Millenium: 'And I will restore thy judges as at the first, and thy counsellors as at the beginning: afterward thou shalt be called, The city of righteousness, the faithfull city' (Isaiah 1,26). Speaking to Parliament on 22 January 1655, Cromwell justified the abolition of the 'hereditary way' of government on the grounds that it was a purging of human institutions and preparation for the Millenium. Considering, he declared, 'that promise in *Isaiah* that God would *give rulers as at the first, and judges as at the beginning*, I did not know but that God might begin, and though at present with a most unworthy person, yet as to the future, it might be after this manner, and I thought this might usher it in'.[11] But whereas Parliament had before it a possible, if by no means unambiguous, model of a Judge, Cowley never proposed a concrete alternative to monarchy. He thought that mankind had fallen again by its choice of monarchy, but he did not suggest any equivalent to Cromwell's Judge, or Hobbes's sovereign power, or Milton's popular sovereignty. Book IV of the *Davideis* is inherently political, since the issues it raises and its mode of argument—appeal to scriptural authority—were both central to political discussion during the period. But its only positive political statement is Samuel's speech to the Israelites about the merits of Saul:

> The *Honour* heav'en has cloath'd him with, sits *fit*
> And comely on him; since you needs must be
> Rule'd by a *King*, you'are happy that 'tis *He*.
> Obey him gladly, and let him too know
> *You* were not made for *Him*, but he for *You*,
> And both for *God*.
> Whose gentlest yoke if once you cast away,
> In vain shall *he* command, and *you* obey.
> To foreign *Tyrants* both shall *slaves* become,
> Instead of *King*, and *Subjects* here at home.   (P, 382)

The half-line—a device Cowley imitated, 'where the sense seems to invite a man to that liberty' (p. 269), from Virgil—makes his main point. His recommendation of limited monarchy, of mutual restraint between subject and ruler, parallels Denham's celebration of Magna Carta:

> Here was that Charter seal'd, wherein the Crown
> All marks of Arbitrary power lays down:
> Tyrant and slave, those names of hate and fear,
> The happier stile of King and Subject bear:
> Happy, when both to the same Center move,
> When Kings give liberty, and Subjects love.[12]

But 'Arbitrary power', of one kind or another, has destroyed this balance and triggered the spiral of 'hate and fear'. The 1642 version of *Coopers Hill* ended with an admonition to kings and subjects to reconcile their differences, and thus with the implication that order and harmony may be restored; the 1655 version, reflecting the victory of Parliament in the civil war, is unreservedly pessimistic, and concludes starkly with the simile of the Deluge:

> Stronger, and fiercer by restraint he roars,
> And knows no bound, but makes his power his shores.

The *Davideis*, similarly, is a work of political despair, the distance between it and *The Civil War* equivalent to the distance between the two versions of *Coopers Hill*. In Cowley's poem, Saul applies to David the image of a 'tame *stream*' which may become 'wild and dangerous' by 'unjust force':

His mutinous waters hurry to the *War*,
And *Troops* of *Waves* come rolling from afar.
Then scorns he such weak stops to his free source,
And overruns the neighboring fields with violent course.

(P, 243)

The final alexandrine enacts an overrunning of limits which Saul himself, rather than David, will exemplify. For Cowley, 'king' and 'tyrant' are virtually synonymous, and Book IV of the *Davideis* can only register the bewilderment of the victim of abused power, caught between the violence of tyranny and the violence of anarchy. Perhaps what one remembers most is Samuel's emphasis on the wilfulness of the Israelites—

But why this yoke on your own necks to draw?
Why *Man* your *God*, and *Passion* made your *Law*?

(P, 371)

—which parallels the stress laid by *The Civil War* on the wilfulness of Charles's enemies. The Israelites have *chosen* tyranny and by that wilful reduction of politics from a divine to an exclusively human scheme deprived themselves of the only lasting solution. Cowley too has argued himself into an impasse, by allowing a problem posed during the course of his poem about 'things *Divine*' to be debated in terms provided by contemporary political discourse and fully intelligible only in that context. The poem's rhetoric at this point (i.e. the tone of Samuel's speech) has come adrift from the epic convention in which it had been so painstakingly embedded.

In Book IV, Cowley opposes to the history of the abuse of power the idealised figure of Jonathan, a man who reconciles '*Courage*' and '*Sweetness*':

In *war* the adverse Troops he does assail,
Like an impet'uous *storm* of *wind* and *Hail*.
In *Peace*, like gentlest *Dew* that does asswage
The *burning Months*, and tempers *Syrius* rage.
Kind as the *Suns* blest *Influence*; and where e're
He comes, *Plenty* and *Joy* attend him there.
To *Help* seems all his *Power*, his *Wealth* to *Give*;
To do much *Good* his *sole Prerogative*.

(P, 377)

Jonathan is the antithesis of a tyrant, exercising power ben-
evolently and claiming only the prerogative of doing 'much *Good*'.
Indeed, Jonathan's bountiful goodness, 'Kind as the *Suns* blest *Influence*', provides an ironic anticipation of Charles II in the first
part of 'Absalom and Achitophel', variously imparting his 'vigorous warmth' to 'Wives and Slaves' (lines 7–9). Significantly, two
details in Cowley's description of Jonathan derive from the celebration of Royalist heroes in Book III of *The Civil War*. There he
had spoken of

> Jermin in whom united does remaine
> All that kind Mothers wishes can containe;   (III, 217–8)

a quality also attributed to Jonathan:

> That *Jonathan* in whom does mixt remain
> All that kind *Mothers* wishes can contain.   (P, 377)

Similarly, his claim for Falkland ('How good a Father, Husband,
Master, Friend!') seems applicable, with slight variation, to Jonathan, the 'tendrest *Husband, Master, Father, Son*'. The elegies for the
Royalist dead in *The Civil War* perform the same function—of
counteracting the forces of evil—as the celebration of Jonathan in
the *Davideis*. Just as the former was split between satire and elegy,
so the latter divides between a realistic appraisal of the abuse of
power and an idealised 'character' of the good leader. Again, each
rhetoric is given an equal emotional, although not of course moral,
weight, so that David presents Samuel's exasperation as forcibly
as Jonathan's virtue; the narrative appears to have lost its grip on
the transcendent *point d'appui* which would enable it to synthesise
those rhetorics, organise them into a hierarchy. That is the situation Cowley had arrived at in Book IV, the last he completed.

II

Book I of the *Davideis* had been most conscientiously devoted to
the establishment of a unifying epic structure which would code
the ensuing sequence of events. Again, the major unifying device is

a cosmology, although this time the account of hell (preserved virtually intact from *The Civil War*) has been balanced by an account of heaven. Thus whatever happens happens within the divine plan and is assured of a proper resolution:

> I Sing the *Man* who *Judahs Scepter* bore
> In that right.hand which held the *Crook* before;
> Who from best *Poet*, best of *Kings* did grow;
> The two chief *gifts Heav'n* could on *Man* bestow.
> Much danger first, much toil did he sustain,
> Whilst *Saul* and *Hell* crost his strong fate in vain.
> Nor did his *Crown* less painful work afford;
> Less exercise his *Patience*, or his *Sword*;
> So long her *Conque'ror Fortunes* spight pursu'd;
> Till with unwearied *Virtue* he subdu'd
> All homebred Malice, and all forreign boasts;
> Their strength was *Armies*, his the *Lord* of *Hosts*.   (P, 242)

Because David is God's champion, his strength is of a different kind from that of his enemies; he does not so much oppose them as assimilate them to a higher level of reality. His triumph over Goliath, like Jonathan's almost single-handed massacre of the Philistines in Book IV, represents such an 'assimilation', plausible in divine but not in human terms. David's fitness for this role was further reinforced by his pious interest in song, a point made by St Augustine in *The City of God*.

But it was not enough for these characters and events to be coded ethically, according to their place in a divine plan. They had also to be proved on the pulse of the reader, rhetorically; in this respect, Cowley learnt from a heathen epic, Virgil's *Aeneid*, which he imitated at every level from specific devices to the parallel drawn between David and Aeneas in Book III. A crucial factor in the writing of Renaissance epic was the need to reconcile two types of coding, or imitation: literary imitation of classical models, and ethical imitation of Christian values.[13] By literary imitation of Virgil, Cowley could provide the sacred truth of his biblical tale with the conviction of an established, indeed widely revered, rhetorical practice. His message would carry weight with the reader because of its conformity to a familiar literary code, a code embodied by the *Aeneid*, which was widely taught in the schools and generally considered to be the greatest of all epics.

Cowley took this programme of literary imitation, of conformity to the classical model, so seriously that he translated the first book of the *Davideis* into Latin, and may even have intended separate publication of the full Latin translation.[14] Virgilian epic represented a pattern into which the history of the Jews could be fitted; it provided a context for events whose significance was not immediately apparent, an assurance of resolution. Cowley's statement in the Preface that he had designed the poem in twelve books, 'not for the *Tribes* sake, but after the *Pattern* of our Master *Virgil*', (P, 11), symbolises this function. However, the problem with the *Davideis*, as with *The Civil War*, was that this unifying structure broke down during the course of the poem. Book IV enters the area of political argument or, as I have suggested, of political despair. It separates into two realities—the inevitable abuse of power, and Jonathan's equally inevitable virtue—which oppose each other on level terms; there is little sense that one will include or assimilate the other, and thus provide a resolution. Rather, they will continue to oppose each other, because political despair has become for Cowley as much of a reality as the virtue of God's champions.

The reason for the collapse of unifying structure can be sought at the very base of the poem, in the fact that it is an epic with footnotes. 'If', Johnson wrote, 'the continuation of the *Davideis* can be missed, it is for the learning that had been diffused over it, and the notes in which it had been explained'.[15] The most interesting notes are those concerned with the status of the narrative, and in particular with its refusal to leave the realm of fable and become history. Throughout, Cowley reveals considerable anxiety about the probability of his narrative. For example, Envy's speech in Book I raises questions as to how Cain killed Abel, and as to the manner of Corah's punishment for rebelling against Moses ('the ground clave asunder that was under them', Numbers 17, 31), and Cowley has two notes on these points:

16 . . . We must . . . be content to be ignorant of the cause, since it hath pleased God not to declare it; neither is it declared in what manner he slew his *Brother*: And therefore I had the Liberty to chuse that which I thought most probable; which is, that he knockt him on the head with some great stone, which was one of the first ordinary and most natural weapons of Anger . . .

17 Though the *Jews* used to bury, and not to Burn the Dead, yet it is very probable that some Nations, even so anciently, practised Burning of them, and that is enough to make it allowable for the *Fury* here to allude to that custom: which if we believe *Statius*, was received even among the *Graecians* before the *Theban War*. (P, 270–1)

Cowley interpolates his own version of events, 'that which I thought most probable', filling a lacuna in the biblical text. But there is always the additional process of the footnote, justifying the liberties taken with the original text. One thus has two types of statement, narrative and footnote, which function according to different criteria of truth. The narrative relates, the footnotes certify; one convinces by the force and beauty of its rhetoric, the other by an appeal to factual evidence.

The possibility of the two types of statement contradicting each other increases wherever Cowley, instead of claiming that the narrative at a particular point is probable, admits its improbability, but argues that what is said should be taken 'in a Poetical sense' (Book I, note 11, P, 268). Thus, he gives the opinions of various commentators about Isaac's age, but decides that, for his own purposes, Isaac ought to be imagined as youthful: 'The *Painters* commonly make him very young, and my description agrees most with that opinion, for it is more poetical and pathetical than the others' (Book II, note 28, P, 311). Or again: 'This particular of *Jagal* and *Davids* going in disguise into the Land of the *Philistims* . . . is added to the History by a *Poetical Licence*, which I take to be very harmless, and which therefore I make bold to use upon several occasions' (Book III, note 5, P, 352). Or again, for a piece of battleground lore: 'That *Naas* was slain in this battel, I have *Josephus* his authority; that *Jonathan* slew him, is a *stroke* of *Poetry*' (Book IV, note 37, P, 399). What is remarkable is not that Cowley should indulge in poetical licence, or strokes of poetry, but that he should feel obliged to justify his indulgences. The criterion of factual evidence is a second voice which speaks in the poem, forcing him to admit that what may be valid at one level—'in a Poetical sense'—is not necessarily valid at another. The narrative attempts to persuade the reader of its probability by a use of language and a description of events proper to heroic poetry, while the footnotes persistently suggest an alternative criterion: factual evidence. The two types of statement move into conflict.

The seventeenth century witnessed the gradual but steady replacement of one set of criteria for the discovery and articulation of truth by another, a process which one can see happening, for example, in rhetorical theory. Traditionally, rhetoricians had distinguished between two methods of persuasion: artistic, and non-artistic proof. Aristotle had written that, of the methods of persuasion,

> some belong strictly to the art of rhetoric and some do not. By the latter I mean such things as are not supplied by the speaker but are there at the outset—witnesses, evidence given under torture, written contracts, and so on. By the former I mean such as we can ourselves construct by means of the principles of rhetoric. The one kind has merely to be used, the other has to be invented.

Artistic procedures require the speaker to create conviction by rhetorical means, by a persuasive eloquence; he must appeal to collateral facts which, in the experience of mankind, are normally accepted as proof of the fact at issue. Non-artistic procedures involve the exploitation of evidence such as that provided by eye-witnesses, which has nothing to do with the rhetorical skill of the advocate or with the collective experience of mankind. Ramus echoed Aristotle in distinguishing between the two types of argument:

> Argument then is artistic or non-artistic, as Aristotle partitions it in the second of the *Rhetoric*: artistic, which creates belief by itself and by its nature, is divided into the primary and the derivative primary.

> Non-artistic argument is that which by itself and through its own force does not create belief, as for example the five types which Aristotle describes in the first of his *Rhetoric*, laws, witnesses, contracts, tortures, oaths. Thus it is always that these arguments are interchangeably called authorities and witnesses.[16]

The distinction is between a system which creates conviction 'by itself and through its own force', and one which requires no intervention on the part of the speaker. Artistic proofs, as Howell puts it, were so called because they were 'developed by systematic means from all of the truths already known and accepted about all the patterns of behavior involved in any case handled by rhetoric,' whereas non-artistic proofs had merely to be used if they existed or ignored if they didn't. Ramus's method consisted of ten places or seats of argument, nine of which produced artistic proofs, whereas the tenth was a provision to take care of any non-artistic proofs that might exist; fifty-five pages of the *Dialectique* were devoted to artistic proof, and five to non-artistic proof. In the course of the seventeenth century this emphasis was decisively reversed. An age which was rapidly developing facilities for the study and dissemination of factual evidence was bound to pay more attention to non-artistic proof. Howell discerns, throughout the seventeenth century, a 'disposition on the part of some writers to turn away from a rhetoric of invention by commonplace and to adopt a rhetoric of invention by research.' This shift of emphasis seems also to have taken place within legal practice as well as within rhetorical theory, and the category of non-artistic proof itself did not remain stable. As Christopher Hill has pointed out, oaths (which Ramus included under non-artistic proofs) were beginning to lose their almost sacred validity:

> In the sixteenth and seventeenth centuries the society in which the sworn jury of presentment was a crucial institution in maintaining law and order (and in which oaths were rejected only by heretics and rebels) was yielding place to a business society in which modern laws of evidence were becoming possible. The jury was being transformed from a group of knowing neighbours to a panel of anonymous citizens presumed to be objective because ignorant. In this society oaths lost their force because self-interest obliged. Legal processes themselves, like religion, came to turn less on correct repetition of the appropriate formulae, more on consideration of intention.[17]

Again, the reliance on familiar ritualised signs of truth has been superseded by a greater concern for the specific facts of the case. It was this shift of emphasis which led Hobbes to formulate his distinction between 'locutionary truth' and 'propositional truth'; a distinction which, as I have suggested, had direct consequences for literature.[18] Cowley's animus against fables depending (like Livy's account of the talkative cow) on 'faith in men only' was fostered by, indeed only made possible by, the emergence of a new criterion of truth.

But Cowley did not in fact banish fable from the *Davideis*, any more than Hobbes banished faith from the *Leviathan*. There is rather, in both cases, a division between types of statement: narrative and footnotes, knowledge or science and eschatology. I have already pointed out that Cowley was obliged to create a category of spoken truth, of statements to be taken 'in a Poetical sense' only. There are times when the poem will only work as it were by artistic proof, by a reliance on the way things have always been said rather than on factual evidence. Hence the significance of the programme of literary imitation of the *Aeneid*, which represented the most important available model of epic statement. At one point Cowley flouts biblical authority in order to introduce a detail which has a splendid Virgilian precedent:

> The Scripture does not say particularly, that *Abram* surprised this Army in, or after a debauch, but it is probable enough for my turn, that this was the case. Of these *Confused marks of death and luxury*, there is an excellent description in the 9. Aeneid, where *Nisus* and *Eurialus* fall upon the quarter of the Enemy.
> (Book II, note 20, P, 309)

Cowley's sense of the need to record what was actually the case makes him acknowledge his divergence from the biblical text. But he is writing an epic poem, not history, and can therefore appeal to the criteria governing another type of statement or spoken truth ('excellent description'). The footnote, itself a locus of known truth, forces into the open a division between two types of statement; it demonstrates that the poet, like Hobbes's parrot, may say something without knowing whether or not it is actually true.

In the instance I have just quoted, the two types of statement coexist, if rather uneasily. But coexistence could easily become an absolute division, a virtual splitting of the poem from itself. Thus, Cowley's description of heaven in Book I draws heavily on a traditional cosmology:

> Above the subtle foldings of the Sky,
> Above the well-set *Orbs* soft *Harmony*,
> Above those petty *Lamps* that guild the *Night*;
> There is a place o'reflown with hallowed *Light*;

Where *Heaven*, as if it left it self behind,
Is stretcht out far, nor its own *bounds* can find:
Here *peaceful Flames* swell up the sacred place,
Nor can the glory contain it self in th' endless space.

(P, 250–1)

Heaven, within the scheme of the poem, stands in contrast with hell, a place of '*Solid* darkness', of 'tyr'anous and unquestion'd *Night*'. But Cowley's awareness of the claims of known truth ('*knowledge* or *science*') undermines the sufficiency of these rhetorical oppositions; any account of the world must be validated by the equivalent of non-artistic proofs. So he adds a most revealing footnote:

> In this, and some like places, I would not have the Reader judge of my opinion by what I say; no more than before in divers expressions about *Hell*, the *Devil*, and *Envy*. It is enough that the Doctrine of the *Orbs*, and the *Musick* made by their motion had been received very anciently, and probably came from the *Eastern* parts; for *Pythagoras* (who first brought this into *Greece*) learnt there most of his *Philosophy*. And to speak according to common opinion, though it be false, is so far from being a fault in Poetry, that it is the custom even of the Scripture to do so; and that not only in the Poetical pieces of it; as where it attributes the *members* and *passions* of mankind to *Devils, Angels*, and God himself; where it calls the *Sun* and *Moon* the two *Great Lights*, whereas the latter is in truth one of the smallest; but is spoken of, as it *seems*, not as it *Is*, and in too many other places to be collected here.
>
> (Note 24, P, 272)

He adds further examples from Virgil and Statius, the second of which, he says, 'is false, but so well said, that it were ill changed for the *Truth*'. His own account of heaven and hell is developed, to paraphrase Howell's definition of artistic proof, from all of the truths already known and accepted about the cosmological pattern involved in heroic poetry; it relies on what Hobbes would call 'faith in men only'. But such an account describes things as they seem, or are traditionally thought to be, not as they really are, and this alternative criterion of known truth forces a damaging retraction: 'I would not have the Reader judge of my opinion by what I say'. Cowley denies the authority of his own poem.

A few lines further on, he celebrates the timeless perfection of heaven:

> On no smooth *Sphear* the restless *seasons* slide,
> No circling *Motion* doth swift *Time* divide;
> Nothing is there *To come*, and nothing *Past*,
> But an *Eternal Now* does always last.   (P, 251)

The last line has the following footnote:

> *Eternity* is defined by *Boet. Lib.* 5. *de Consolat. Interminabilis vitae tota simul & perfecta possessio.* The whole and perfect possession, ever all at once, of a Being without beginning or ending. Which *Definition* is followed by *Tho. Aquin.* and all the *Schoolmen*; who therefore call *Eternity Nunc stans*, a *standing Now*, to distinguish it from that *Now*, which is a difference of *time*, and is alwaies *in Fluxu.*   (Note 26, P, 273)

The definition of eternity as a '*standing Now*', deriving from Augustine as well as from Boethius and Aquinas, was generally accepted during the Renaissance.[19] But it came under severe attack during the time Cowley was engaged on the *Davideis*, occurring for example in the bitter debate on free-will between Hobbes and Bishop Bramhall. 'But he adds', Hobbes wrote,

> that we must subject them, [liberty and necessity] according to that *presentiality* which they have in eternity, which he says cannot be done by them that conceive *eternity* to be an *everlasting succession*, but only by them that conceive it as an *indivisible point*. To which I answer, that as soon as I can conceive it as an *indivisible point*, or anything but an *everlasting succession*, I will renounce all that I have written on this subject. I know St. Thomas Aquinas calls *eternity, nunc stans*, an *everabiding now*; which is easy enough to say, but though I fain would, yet I could never conceive it: they that can, are more happy than I.

Eternity for Hobbes is an infinite prolongation, as Pocock puts it, of the time we know, and this 'determination to acknowledge no processes outside the world of matter, space and time' links Hobbes's thought to the millenarianism of the Puritan sects, and to Milton:

There is certainly no reason why we should conform to the popular belief that motion and time, which is the measure of motion, could not, according to our concepts of 'before' and 'after', have existed before this world was made. For Aristotle, who taught that motion and time are inherent only in this world, asserted, nevertheless, that this world was eternal.

He made the same point in *Paradise Lost*:

> For time, though in Eternitie, appli'd
> To motion, measures all things durable
> By present, past, and future.

For both Milton and Hobbes time and motion pervade eternity, which cannot therefore be the *nunc stans* described by Aquinas and incorporated by Cowley into the *Davideis*. The Catholic tradition, as Pocock puts it, had stressed the synchronic rather than the diachronic presentation of God's relation to men, so that 'instead of human salvation being brought about by a succession of acts performed by the eternal upon the world in time, it appeared rather in terms of a passage of numbers of souls through time to eternity'; a passage performed through the actions of pure grace institutionalised in the rituals of the Church. Thus, the medieval Church 'rested largely upon the minimisation of the eschatological perspective and the diversion of attention from the historical to the institutional; its philosophy correspondingly dealt in terms of the intelligibility of timeless universals in which part of God's reality was accessible to human reason'.[20] Similarly, Cowley's description of heaven was meant to establish a timeless frame of reference which might include and order the flux of historical experience, and so bring events to a proper resolution. Thus, 'by a succession of acts performed by the eternal upon the world in time', David would triumph over his enemies. The cosmology was in a sense 'institutional', a structure of traditional beliefs designed to incorporate and direct individual experience, and Cowley's extensive imitation of Virgil's timeless epic served to further embed the *Davideis* in a frame of reference outside history. The poem represents a most ambitious attempt to sustain the criterion of 'locutionary truth'. But the ground was moving beneath Cowley's feet, and it was Hobbes rather than Crashaw who had the last word: 'I would not have the Reader judge of my opinion by what I say; no more than before in divers expressions about *Hell*, the *Devil*, and *Envy*'.

6 The Pindaric Odes

I

This was not, of course, the end of the story. *Paradise Lost* certainly employed the conventions of 'locutionary truth' to some effect, relying without too many qualms on the credibility of the 'person propounding'. But Cowley went another way; unable to ignore the Hobbesian theory of knowledge, he made a brave effort to respond positively to a conceptual innovation whose radicalism unsettled most of his contemporaries. The very scepticism which sabotaged the *Davideis* became the principle on which the innovatory form of the *Pindarique Odes* was based. Cowley has never got the credit he deserves for this bold change of direction.

According to Thomas Sprat, Cowley encountered the works of Pindar accidentally, 'in a place, where he had no other Books to direct him'. Nethercot identifies this place as Jersey, where Cowley went in 1651 to raise funds for the Queen.[1] Although one doubts whether this was literally the first time Cowley had read Pindar, it may well have been the point at which he decided to employ a Pindaric form in his own verse. The result, at any rate, was the remaining section of the 1656 *Poems*, translations of two odes by Pindar and of Horace's praise of Pindar, and twelve original odes. He thought that his Pindaric experiment was unusual enough to require an additional explanatory Preface:

> I have in these two *Odes* of *Pindar* taken, left out, and added what I please; nor make it so much my aim to let the Reader know precisely what he spoke, as what was his *way* and *manner* of speaking; which has not been yet (that I know of) introduced into *English*, though it be the noblest and highest kind of writing in Verse; and which might, perhaps, be put into the List of *Pancirollus*, among the *lost Inventions* of *Antiquity*.   (P, 156)

There is in the claim that Pindarism represents the 'noblest and highest kind of writing in Verse' a bravado compensating for the failed grandiloquence of the *Davideis*; the focus of Cowley's ambition has shifted. He does not intend to translate specific messages ('precisely what he spoke'), but rather to reinvent a code ('his *way* and *manner* of speaking') which will enable him to say things he could not otherwise have said.

Ben Jonson was the only English poet before Cowley to make a serious attempt to domesticate Pindar, and his 'To the Immortal Memorie, and Friendship of that Noble Paire, Sir Lucius Cary, and Sir H. Morison', published in *Under-Woods* (1640), was the only correct Pindaric ode written during the seventeenth century. Jonson emphasised the special nature of his poem by reproducing the triadic structure of Pindar's odes, and labelling the elements Turn (strophe), Counter-Turn (antistrophe), and Stand (epode), and he also imitated Pindar's abrupt and inconstant style of argument, introducing into the first four stanzas material with no obvious relevance to Morison's death. Pindar's sudden digressions held considerable fascination for seventeenth-century commentators, and Jonson was no exception; his poem digressed abruptly to include the story of a 'Stirrer' (stanza 3). But the ode reverts, with the account of Morison's death in stanza 5, to characteristically Jonsonian preoccupations and techniques, celebrating Morison's integrity. Jonson used a Pindaric form because he felt that its stringent technical demands would reflect the constancy of the relationship he was describing, and, throughout the poem, even where the sense runs on from one stanza to the next, the line-ending is like a scarp:

> Hee leap'd the present age,
> Possest with holy rage,
> To see that bright eternall Day:
> Of which we *Priests*, and *Poets* say
> Such truths, as we expect for happy men,
> And there he lives with memorie; and *Ben*
>
> *Jonson*, who sung this of him, e're he went
> Himselfe to rest . . .

The poet's surname, straddling the gap between stanzas, acts as a hinge, and one feels that each stanza is a compact unit to be fitted into a stable structure. This notion of Pindaric form together with the prominence given to the act of naming embodies Jonson's ethical design:

> You liv'd to be the great surnames,
> And titles, by which all made claimes
> Unto the Vertue. Nothing perfect done,
> But as a CARY, or a MORISON.[2]

Cary and Morison have given virtue an emblematic form, and Jonson's poem will complete the process by placing these emblems within a ceremonial order, the order of metre and rhyme (notice his association of '*Poets*' with '*Priests*'). The ceremonial order, aspiring to the fixity and permanence of emblem, is sustained by a firm cadence, by an extensive use of couplets in preference to a more flexible scheme, and by strong, monosyllabic line-endings which assert a boundary. Pindaric inconstancy of argument obviously runs counter to this emphasis, and although Jonson did introduce an element of inconstancy, he was not able to follow it through. Nor does the shift from a digressive to a more concentrated procedure mark any kind of development in the poem's moral scheme; Jonson simply abandons a recognised element of Pindaric style which happens to obstruct rather than to further his purpose.

The term seventeenth-century commentators used to define the element of Pindaric style which Jonson recognised but could not accommodate was 'hardiness'. Blondel, in his *Comparison of Pindar and Horace*, remarked that Pindar's odes contain 'some Fashions of speaking so hardy, and so far from our common use, that a Man can hardly consider of them, without finding them ridiculous'. Hardiness here seems to denote an unfamiliar use of language and the term was given a different but compatible sense by Basil Kennett, who defended Pindar against attacks on the 'unaccountable Digressions and the furious rambles of his Wit' with the following argument: 'The common Answer to this Impeachment is drawn from the nature of Pindar's way of Writing: this Libertinism of Conduct being the very Life and Soul of his Pieces . . . It's plain *Pindar* was sensible of his hardiness, in wandring so loosely from the main Subject'.[3] For Kennett, hardiness involves inconstancy of argument, but one imagines that it was precisely this inconstancy which the seventeenth-century reader would have found most unfamiliar. Cowley's Preface to the 1656 *Poems* encompasses both senses of hardiness:

> For as for the *Pindarick Odes* (which is the third part) I am in great doubt whether they will be understood by most *Readers*; nay, even by very many who are well enough acquainted with the common Roads, and ordinary Tracks of *Poesie* . . . The digressions are many, and sudden, and sometimes long, according to the fashion of all *Lyriques*, and of *Pindar* above all men living.   (P, 10–11)

He was, then, quite deliberately developing a poetic which ran contrary to the expectations of his readership, and which placed great emphasis on the element of inconstancy, an element Jonson's more traditional poetic had not been able to accommodate. Indeed, he went on to underline the strangeness of the Pindaric style:

> The *Figures* are unusual and *bold*, even to *Temeritie*, and such as I durst not have to do withal in any other kind of *Poetry*: The *Numbers* are various and irregular, and sometimes (especially some of the long ones) seem harsh and uncouth, if the just measures and cadencies be not observed in the *Pronunciation*. So that almost all their *Sweetness* and *Numerosity* (which is to be found, if I mistake not, in the roughest, if rightly repeated) lies in a manner wholly at the *Mercy* of the *Reader*.

Cowley dwells on the '*Temeritie*' of his odes and, by an interesting manoeuvre, shifts the responsibility for a proper reading from poet to reader. The odes represent an abnormal vision, which the reader must adjust or fit himself to as best he can, rather than the other way round.

What, then, was the purpose of this induction into an unfamiliar literary experience? What did Cowley hope to achieve by stylistic hardiness? So far, only one critic, Harvey Goldstein, has proposed a plausible answer to these questions.[4] Goldstein argues that the theory of *discordia concors* provided the kind of literary context in which a Pindaric style could be developed; a theory developed, he says, by rhetoricians, defenders of scriptural style, Italian *concettisti*, and English poets writing 'strong lines'. But I think one has to distinguish between the two prominent features, in seventeenth-century eyes, of Pindaric style: *extravagance* of metre and imagery, and *hardiness* (or difficult and inconstant argument). There was indeed, as Goldstein claims, a stylistic consensus favouring extravagance of metre and imagery; the evidence lies in the 'strong lines' argument, in the hyperbolic imagery of *The Mistress,* and in the commendatory poems to Sandys' paraphrase of the Psalms, which he cites. Rhetorical tradition had, furthermore, always encompassed a concept of rugged style. Dionysius of Helicarnassus used Pindar as an example 'in lyric poetry' of 'austere'—as opposed to 'smooth or (florid)' and 'harmoniously blended'—composition. After quoting some verses by Pindar, he commented that 'these lines are vigorous, weighty and dignified, and possess much austerity; . . . though rugged, they are not unpleasantly so, and though harsh to the ear, are but so in due measure'. But he avoided the issue of inconstancy of argument; indeed, it is difficult to see how any rhetoric could accommodate a style that was thought to be systematic only in its irregularity. Since the reader has to abandon his literary preconceptions in order to read Cowley's odes, their austerity would seem to exceed any notion of 'due measure' or decorum, and I do not think that, in 1650, any established decorum would have favoured hardiness. The real problem, which could not be resolved by any established decorum, was that, as Dryden remarked, Pindar 'is known to be a dark writer, to want connection (I mean as to our understanding), to soar out of sight, and leave his reader at a gaze'.[5]

Such a decorum, justifying want of connection, did not become available until 1674 at the earliest, when Boileau translated the *Peri Hypsous* of 'Longinus'. It was not the translation which had radical consequences, so much as Boileau's preface and the *Réflexions critiques sur quelques passages du rhéteur Longin* which followed in 1694 and 1713. Boileau distinguished between the Sublime and a sublime style, and thus removed the aesthetic sublime altogether from the field of rhetoric, or indeed from any system of empirical classification. He understood the Sublime not as the style suited to a particular kind of subject-matter or designed to produce a particular effect, but as something more than that, as whatever is surprising 'dans le discours'. The *Peri Hypsous* had been available for a long time before Boileau's translation, but it had been regarded as a rhetorical handbook, and valued for its exposition of stylistic propriety. The definition of wit in Cowley's 'Of Wit' parallels the Longinan account of sublimity, but the 'most original suggestion of *Peri Hypsous*, that the sublime was impossible where there was no passion, that its effect was not persuasion but transport, found no place in Cowley's short definition'.[6] Until Boileau explained 'discours' in non-rhetorical terms, there was no basis for a stylistic decorum which would encompass either Pindar or the Sublime. (Not surprisingly, he defended Pindar against the criticisms of Perrault in the eighth of his *Réflexions critiques*.) The notion of the Sublime had, as is well known, a very important effect on eighteenth-century English criticism. It encouraged, notably in Addison, a tendency to shun mediocre talents, and to praise most highly those authors like Shakespeare and Milton whose work, despite lapses from propriety, revealed spectacular beauties.[7] Addison included Pindar in the second category, because he was 'a great Genius of the first Class, who was hurried on by a natural Fire and Impetuosity to vast Conceptions of things, and noble Sallies of Imagination'. The new criticism assimilated Pindarism as well into an aesthetic of irregularity. Addison even recommended Pindaric horticulture, claiming that 'my Compositions in Gardening are altogether after the *Pindarick* manner, and run into the beautiful Wildness of Nature, without affecting the nicer Elegancies of Art'. The '*Pindarick* manner' of gardening would appear to accommodate irregularity, inconstant development, discontinuity: 'I . . . am pleased when I am walking in a Labyrinth of my own raising, not to know whether the next Tree I shall meet with is an Apple or an Oak, an Elm or a Pear-tree'.[8] Hardiness and lack of connection, which Cowley enshrined in the theory of Pindarism, exceed the regulated disharmony of *discordia concors*, and the first four *Pindarique Odes* emphasise this element of the theory. 'The *Ode*', he said of the Second Olympian, '(according to the constant custom of the *Poet*) consists more in *Digressions*, than in the main *subject*' (P, 157); a remark which tends to invalidate any such distinction between digression and main subject. Describing the First Nemean, Cowley stressed Pindar's 'usual manner of being transported with any good Hint that meets him in his way' (P, 170); translating Horace's account of the 'swoln *Flood*' of Pindar's verse, he interpolated the adjective 'unnavigable' (P, 178). Genius, according to the *Peri Hypsous*, 'needs the curb as often as the spur',[9] but Cowley's 'The Resurrection' proclaims the independence of the

Pindaric muse from both:

> 'Tis an unruly, and a *hard-Mouth'd Horse*,
> Fierce, and unbroken yet,
> Impatient of the *Spur* or *Bit*.   (P, 183)

Control resides not with any external decorum or prescription, but with the mutual sensitivity of poet and audience; the ode 'flings *Writer* and *Reader* too that *sits* not *sure*'. 'The Resurrection', as Cowley noted, 'is truly *Pindarical*, falling from one thing into another, after his *Enthusiastical manner*'. These first four odes define and implement a poetic whose main feature is hardiness: difficulty and lack of connection.

II

The basis for that poetic lies, I believe, in the equivalence between Cowley's version of the Pindaric ode and the radical psychology developed by Thomas Hobbes, who, unlike the various theorists cited by Goldstein, knew Cowley well, possibly at Great Tew and certainly at Paris, during the years immediately prior to the composition of the *Pindarique Odes*. His theory of mind derived its most important and radical assumption from the Galilean theory of inertial motion, with which he had become familiar during the 1630s. Aristotle had regarded motion as the resolution of an internal tension between the potential and actual states of a person or object; it was thus a form of self-realisation, the discovery of an essential 'whatness' or true place in the order of things. Such striving towards fulfilment, from potentiality to actuality, was a form of motion inherent in both the physical and the moral worlds. Hobbes, following Galileo, defined motion as a consequence of the external relations between objects, rather than of an evaluative tension within them. Once in motion, an object would continue to move not until its essential nature had been revealed, but until prevented from doing so by a contrary force. Hobbes applied this concept of inertial motion to the working of the mind. The Will, he thought, was simply the last of a series of forces or appetites, and not a faculty in tension with Right Reason. Discourse, similarly, was ordered by the external relations between concepts or impressions, relations which might be quite arbitrary. Indeed,

Hobbes introduced a special term in order to accommodate the possible arbitrariness of discourse. The '*succession* of conceptions in the mind', he wrote, may be '*casual* and incoherent, as in dreams for the most part', or they may be '*orderly*, as when the former thought introduceth the latter; and this is *discourse* of the mind. But because the word discourse is commonly taken for the *coherence* and consequence of words, I will, to avoid equivocation, call it *discursion*'. Since Hobbes considered the genesis of all concepts to be in the senses, the order of 'discursion' must depend on the possibly fortuitous external relations between sense impressions. The succession of conceptions in the mind, he wrote, is caused 'by the succession they *had* one to another when they were produced by the *senses*'; and 'it must needs follow, that one *conception* followeth *not* another, according to our election, and the need we have of them, *but* as it *chanceth* us to hear or see such things as shall bring them to our mind'. No immanent pattern is revealed by the way in which the mind arrives at a conclusion, no tension is resolved, no principle of order vindicated; for this process does not depend upon 'election' or moral choice so much as upon the arbitrary sequence of perceptions experienced at a particular time in a particular place. Hobbes's theory of the association of ideas put in question the very possibility of a teleological frame of reference, emphasising as it did the succession of mental phenomena, rather than the placing of those phenomena within a system of values. Like all the other manifestations of a mechanistic attitude, it aroused opposition. Thomas Manningham, for example, directed a 'Discourse Concerning Truth' against those exponents of 'Modern Scepticism' who 'are so vigorous for the evidence of *Sense*, that they scarce allow any other, but make the most sublimated *Knowledge* a *Tumult* of *Phantasms*; all *Thought, Local Motion*; all *Reason, Mechanism*; and the whole *Encyclopede* of *Arts* and *Sciences* but a *brisker Circulation* of the *Blood*'.[10] 'Local motion' was the technical term used by contemporary scientists to designate inertial motion, and the reduction of thought-processes to local motion was clearly problematic for anyone who held to a traditional psychology. By the time Hobbes came to write the *Leviathan*, he was more interested in 'orderly' than in 'casual' discursion, but he still considered both modes to be equally natural, and indeed common. Cowley's account of the nature and function of the Pindaric ode is not all that far from Manningham's '*Tumult* of *Phantasms*', and the abnormal vision for which the reader was prepared by that account did indeed concern itself primarily with cognition rather than evaluation.

Words, for Hobbes and for Cowley, were pictures of conceptions, and it followed that what applied to the succession of mental conceptions must also apply to language. Cowley's interest in Pindar's inconstancy of argument is, I would suggest, equivalent to Hobbes's interest in discursion. Thus, Cowley's account of Pindar's habit of being transported with any good hint that 'meets him in his way' stresses the arbitrary nature of Pindaric discursion, as indeed does his description of 'The Resurrection' as 'falling from one thing into another'. He was in this respect extrapolating from Pindar's own practice, and his transformation of the ode can best be illustrated by reference to a distinction in Greek lyric poetry, made by Plato and elaborated by Maurice Bowra, between 'choral song' and 'monody'. Choral song was 'in origin and character largely religious', and the choral poet 'gave voice to the traditional and accepted meaning which a feast had for its participants'. It was thus a mode of 'locutionary truth', and its stanzas were normally longer than those of monody, perhaps in order to accommodate the element of dance. The writers of monody, on the other hand, 'speak without reserve of their innermost feelings and do not attempt to identify themselves with their company, or to speak for anyone but themselves'.[11] Pindar wrote choral songs; even his frequent personal remarks have a public context. He 'gave voice', as Bowra says, to traditional and accepted truths, and his function, like any exponent of 'locutionary truth', was to reconcile his audience to their place in the order of things. But Cowley's appeal to the reader to abandon his preconceptions and adapt himself to an idiosyncratic poetic would argue against any such concept of the poet's proper function, and the *Pindarique Odes* were primarily concerned with discursion rather than ceremony. Neglecting the public context of the Pindaric ode, he transformed it into monody.

Bowra's distinction between choral song and monody has been broadened into a contrast between the 'architectural' exposition of ideas—the arrangement of thought in blocks according to strophe or triad—and linear or 'cursive' exposition.[12] Pindar's odes tended towards an 'architectural' exposition, and towards formal symmetry, whereas Cowley's interest in 'cursive' exposition—the development of thought through associative links—is obvious. Cowley discarded the most explicitly ceremonial feature of the Pindaric ode—the strophe-antistrophe-epode structure which accommodated it to the dance—and his stanzas are of indefinite length, the odes themselves sometimes ending abruptly. The state of rest, in the Aristotelian universe, carried strong associations of fulfilment; it was the resolution of a tension between potentiality and actuality, the attainment of a true place in the order of things. For Hobbes, on the other hand, it was not so privileged: an arbitrary interruption of the chain of cause and effect rather than an elected self-realisation. 'And in the chain of discourse', he wrote flatly, 'wheresoever it be interrupted, there is an end for that time'.[13] The difference can be stated in terms of the development of a poem. George Herbert's lyrics—even one as structurally irregular as 'The Collar'—conclude when the poet's errant or rebellious intelligence has been brought to a recognition of its responsibility to God. The development of the poem resolves a moral tension between the false self exhibited by the superficial rhetoric of human reason and the real self discovered by devotion to God, revealing to Herbert his true place in the order of things. Cowley's odes, on the other hand, and 'The Resurrection' is a good example here, tend to be not only irregular in their development but also arbitrary in their conclusion.

The same irregularity is evident in the organisation of individual stanzas, and in Cowley's versification as a whole. Irregular verse, as Robert Shafer points out, 'had made its appearance in English many years before 1656, and had been written occasionally by a long line of English poets before Cowley took it up and made it a fashionable thing'.[14] But Cowley's originality did not lie only in the consistency with which he employed an irregular verse-form, for he developed it not, like previous poets, as a mode of prayer or song, but as a mode of discursion. Irregular verse, like the human mind in Hobbes's account, was not committed to the fulfilment of immanent pattern, and could therefore be adapted to the detours and associative jumps of mental process. It surprised and unsettled the reader by its inconstancy, rather than restoring him to a sense of order. 'I am sorry', Cowley wrote in a footnote to a line in the *Davideis*,

> that it is necessary to admonish the most part of *Readers*, that it is not by *negligence* that this verse is so loose, long, and as it were, *Vast*; it is to paint in the number the nature of the thing which it describes, which I would have observed in divers other places of

this *Poem*, that else will pass for very careless verses . . . The thing is, that the disposition of words and numbers should be such, as that out of the order and sound of them, the things themselves may be represented.   (P, 273)

This representation of 'the things themselves' by the 'disposition of words and numbers', which Johnson described as an attempt at an 'improved and scientific' versification, was a consistent feature of Cowley's work, and he included a similar warning in a footnote to a line in the *Pindarique Odes*: 'It is, I hope, needless to admonish any tolerable *Reader*, that it was not negligence or ignorance of *Number*, that produced this *Stumbling Verse*, no more than the other before, *And truly then headlong into the Sea descend*. And several others in my book of the like kind.' (P, 217) Since the Pindaric ode pursues unexpected connections, 'falling from one thing into another', its measure must be constructed as it develops, giving definition to each conception or discursive unit. Such units are often initiated by short lines and concluded by unusually long ones, and Cowley made considerable use of triplets, because they provided a larger and more flexible unit than the couplet. He seemed to regard the Pindaric ode as a form which subordinated technical considerations to the demands of statement and, on one occasion, after rhyming 'find' with 'refined', he said he would only permit such rhymes in 'this free kind of *Poetry*, and here too very sparingly' (P, 200). 'There can', he continued, 'be no *Musick* with only *one Note*', which implies that the aims of Pindaric versification were not primarily musical. Whole sequences of rhymes do indeed strike a single note—for example, the 'a'-sound in stanza 4 of 'The Muse'—and half-rhymes also occur frequently. Thomas Sprat stressed the flexibility of Pindaric versification and its usefulness as a mode of discursion. 'If the irregularity of the number', he wrote, 'disgust them [Cowley's readers], they may observe that this very thing makes that kind of Poesie fit for all manner of subjects: For the Pleasant, the Grave, the Amorous, the Heroic, the Philosophical, the Moral, the Divine' (*Life*, W, Sig B2 verso). His disregard of decorum—the principle that each type of subject-matter has its appropriate style—shows how the Pindaric ode contravened the traditional way of reading a poem. 'But that', Sprat continued,

for which I think this inequality of number is chiefly to be preferr'd, is its near affinity with Prose: From which all other kinds of *English* Verse are so far distant, that it is very seldom found that the same Man excels in both ways. But now this loose, and unconfin'd measure has all the Grace, and Harmony of the most confin'd. And withal, it is so large and free, that the practice of it will only exalt, not corrupt our Prose: which is certainly the most useful kind of Writing of all others: for it is the Style of all business and conversation.

The passage reflects Sprat's predominant interest in the medium of business and conversation, but it seems to me an accurate enough account of Cowley's intentions.

III

'The Muse', the ode which follows 'The Resurrection', attempts a more extended definition of the expressive function of Pindaric verse. Its first stanza is unremarkable, the kind of discussion of poetry which Hobbes had initiated when he wrote that 'Judgement begets the strength and structure, and Fancy begets the ornaments of a Poem'. Two years later, Edward Benlowes elaborated this distinction:

> Now, 'tis *Judgement* begets the Strength, *Invention* the Ornaments of a Poem; both *These* joyn'd form *Wit*, which is the Agility of Spirits: Vivacity of *Fancie* in a florid Style disposeth Light and Life to a Poem, wherein the Masculine and refined Pleasures of the *Understanding* transcend the feminine and sensual of the *Eye*: From the Excellencie of *Fancie* proceed graceful Similes, apt Metaphors, &c.

Cowley's formulation resembles that of Benlowes quite closely, although, perhaps because the Muse is a queen, he concentrates more on the 'feminine and sensual' pleasures of the eye:

> And let the airy *Footmen* running all beside,
>   Make a long row of *goodly pride*.
> *Figures, Conceits, Raptures*, and *Sentences*
>   In a well-worded *dress*.

And *innocent Loves*, and *pleasant Truths*, and *useful Lies*,
    In all their gaudy *Liveries*.   (P, 185)

But he also gave the masculine pleasures of the understanding
their due, pointing in his note to the first line of the stanza ('Go,
the rich *Chariot* instantly prepare') to a '*Phansie*' which Pindar had
in the Sixth Olympian, where 'he speaks to his own Soul. O, my
Soul, join me the strong and swift *Mules* together, that I may drive
the *Chariot* in this fair way' (P, 186). He also quotes other writers
who had described right reason as the '*Chariot-driver* of the *Soul*',
and the spirits as the '*Chariot* of the Soul'. His primary interest was
in the flight or transport of the understanding, and in the ability of
the poet to encourage and enter into this process. 'Thus', according to the *Peri Hypsous*, 'within the scope of human enterprise there
lie such powers of contemplation and thought that even the whole
universe cannot satisfy them, but our ideas often pass beyond the
limits that enring us'.[15] Although the first stanza is conventional
in its balancing of the masculine and feminine pleasures of poetry,
the second stanza emphasises above all the Muse's ability to 'pass
beyond the limits that enring us'.

Poetry possesses powers of contemplation and thought which
'even the whole universe cannot satisfy':

    Whatever *God* did *Say*,
    Is all thy plain and smooth, uninterrupted *way*.
    Nay ev'n beyond his *works* thy *Voyages* are known,
        Thou 'has thousand *worlds* too of thine *own*.
    Thou speakst, great *Queen*, in the same *stile* as *He*,
    And a *New world* leaps forth when *Thou* say'st, *Let it Be*.

Here, as throughout 'The Muse', Cowley emphasises the sense
of flight or propulsion by starting lines with a verb, launching the
verse powerfully; his frequent use of the copula 'and' in a similar
position gives the stanza momentum, producing surges of
energy. But it is of course the momentum of thought rather than
action, and therefore frictionless—a point made by the subtly
placed caesura in the second line of my quotation, which allows
the rhythm to dip slightly before picking it up again with
polysyllabic assurance. The irregularity of the verse, orientated
towards flexibility and open-endedness rather than the fulfilment of pattern, is crucial to such effects. But the literary doc-

trine developed by Cowley in this stanza resembles quite closely the 'poetic of correspondence' described by Joseph Mazzeo. The Italian theorist Emanuele Tesauro, Mazzeo says, conceived wit as 'the faculty in man analogous to God's creative power. It is a small particle of the divine nature, for it can create 'being' where there was no 'being' before.' Similarly, Cowley declared that the Muse spoke in the same style as God, and amplified the point in a footnote:

> The meaning is, that *Poetry* treats not only of all things that are, or can be, but makes *Creatures* of her own, as *Centaurs, Satyrs, Fairies,* &c. makes *persons* and *actions* of her own, as in *Fables* and *Romances,* makes *Beasts, Trees, Waters,* and other irrational and insensible things to act above the possibility of their natures, as to *understand* and *speak,* nay makes what *Gods* it pleases too without *Idolatry,* and varies all these into innumerable *Systemes,* or *Worlds* of Invention.   (P, 187)

Cowley's concept of poetic invention exceeds the Hobbesian limit of 'conceived possibility', recalling Bacon's statement that poetry goes beyond the 'measure of nature, joining at pleasure things which in nature would never have come together, and introducing things which in nature would never have come to pass'. In this stanza, he also illustrates another feature of the theory of 'metaphysical wit': the construction of elaborate analogies between apparently dissimilar forms of being. He is describing the flight-path of the Muse's chariot:

> Where never *Foot* of *Man,* or *Hoof* of *Beast,*
>   The passage prest,
>   Where never *Fish* did *fly,*
> And with short silver *wings* cut the low liquid *Sky.*
>   Where *Bird* with painted *Oars* did nere
> Row through the trackless *Ocean* of the *Air.*

The passage is, as it were, sprung on its verbs, each of them in a position of metrical prominence either within or at the extremities of the lines. Its wit resides, to adapt Mazzeo's account of metaphysical wit, in 'that quality of vision which the discovery of correspondences can bring, the 'thrill' which the awareness of an analogy gives the intellect when it first becomes aware of the identity between things formerly believed unconnected'. One might compare Cowley's lines with a possible source in Benlowes's *Theophila*:

> LORD, mount me to the Pitch of *Larks* on *High*;
> That I, as *Birds* wing'd Oars, may cut the Skie![16]

Benlowes believed, with tiresome persistence, that piety involved the perception of startling and witty correspondences, and his metaphor was designed to stimulate religious ecstacy. Cowley, one feels, was more interested in the exercise of wit for its own sake, the intellectual 'thrill'.

The second stanza of 'The Muse' moves the discussion on from the 'feminine' to the 'masculine' pleasures of poetry, from a concept of metaphor as ornament to a concept of metaphor as the discovery of hidden connections. By this movement, it in no way exceeds accepted theories of poetic style. But the third stanza, which I shall quote in full, does push the argument further:

> Thou fadom'est the deep *Gulf* of *Ages* past,
>   And canst pluck up with ease
> The *years* which Thou dost please,
> Like shipwrackt *Treasures* by rude *Tempests* cast
>   Long since into the *Sea*,
> Brought up again to *light* and publique *Use* by Thee.
>   Nor dost thou onely *Dive* so low,
>   But *Fly*
> With an unwearied *Wing* the other way on high,
>   Where *Fates* among the *Stars* do grow;
> There into the close *Nests* of *Time* do'st peep,
>   And there with piercing *Eye*,
> Through the firm *shell*, and the thick *White* do'st spie,
>   *Years to come* a forming lie,
> Close in their *sacred Secondine* asleep,
>   Till *hatcht* by the *Suns* vital heat
>   Which o're them yet does *brooding* set
>   They *Life* and *Motion* get,
>   And *ripe* at last with vigorous might
> Break through the *Shell*, and take their everlasting *Flight*.

Again one notices the prominence of monosyllabic verbs, particularly in the concluding couplet, where the turn of the line enacts the eruption it describes. Cowley unfolds the correspondence established metaphorically in the previous stanza, between fish and bird; one element (sea) represents the past, the other (sky) the future. His concern is not simply with the intellectual 'thrill' provided by a poetic of correspondence, and the purpose of imaginative flight turns out to be knowledge rather than worship. '*Antiquities*, or remnants of histories', Bacon had written, 'are . . . like the spars of a shipwreck; when, though the memory of things be decayed and almost lost, yet acute and industrious persons, by a certain persevering and scrupulous diligence, contrive . . . to recover somewhat from the deluge of time'. Cowley's poetic equivalent of this salvage-operation is less laborious, but its ends are suitably Baconian, for the poetic imagination recovers past events 'to *light* and publique *Use*', a dual purpose which recalls Bacon's distinction between 'experiments of Light' and 'experiments of Fruit'. Poetry, furthermore, also ascends with 'unwearied *Wing* the other way on high, / Where *Fates* among the *Stars* do grow', and Bacon, although distrusting the wilder sort of astrological speculation, did believe that it was possible to predict future events by observing the positions of the stars. He prescribed four approaches to a 'reformed' or 'sane' astrology: by future experiments, by past experiments, by traditions and by physical reasons:

> Lastly of physical reasons, those are most adapted to this investigation which make inquiry into the universal appetites and passions of matter, and the simple and genuine motions of bodies. For upon these wings we ascend most safely to these celestial material substances.[17]

Cowley, too, was sceptical of astrology and footnoted his reference to the fates growing among the stars with a disclaimer: 'According to the vulgar (but false) opinion of the *Influence* of the *Stars* over mens *actions* and *Fortunes*'. But his account of the process of generation demonstrates his reliance on 'physical reasons', and he certainly prescribes a Baconian ascent to 'celestial material substances'. 'The Muse' has by this time identified poetry with the pursuit of knowledge, delineating an '*open Road*' for both projects.

Poetry extends our knowledge not only of past and future, but also of the present. 'Things', Bacon wrote, 'are preserved and

continued in two ways; either in their own identity, or by repair.
In their own identity, as a fly or an ant in amber; a flower or an
apple or wood in conservatories of snow; a corpse in balsam. By
repair, as in flame, and in things mechanical.'[18] Cowley thought
that the present moment could best be preserved in its own identity, rather than by repair:

> Thou stopst this *Current*, and dost make
> This running *River* settle like a *Lake*,
> Thy certain hand holds fast this slippery *Snake*.
>   The *Fruit* which does so quickly wast,
>   Men scarce can see it, much less *tast*,
> Thou *Comfitest* in *Sweets* to make it *last*.
>   This shining piece of *Ice*
>   Which melts so soon away
>   With the *Suns* ray,
> Thy *Verse* does solidate and *Chrystallize*,
>   Till it a lasting *Mirror* be.
>   Nay thy *Immortal Rhyme*
>   Makes this one short *Point* of *Time*,
> To fill up half the *Orb* of *Round Eternity*.

Cowley attributes to poetry the power of solidating and crystal-
lising experience, of rendering it as stable as a lake or a mirror.
The very device of metaphor confers a stable identity on momentary impressions, by relating them to other and perhaps
more fundamental aspects of experience, while rhythm can also
have a stabilising effect. Thus, the assertions of the solidating
function of verse—'Thou *Comfitest* . . . *last*', 'Thy *Verse* . . .
Chrystallize'—are themselves longer lines anchoring the nervous,
jerkier rhythms of the descriptions of flux. Rhyme, too, pre-
serves identity of sound across the succession of lines, and the
Rhyme/Time coupling expresses this perfectly.

This identification of literary method with cognitive processes
takes 'The Muse' decisively beyond a 'poetic of correspondence', for it was the attitude to knowledge stimulated by
the 'intellectual revolution' which, as Mazzeo says, destroyed
the assumptions underlying that poetic. The theory of
'Metaphysical' wit described by Mazzeo and by S. L. Bethell
was concerned with the discovery or intuition of witty correspondences in the universe, and such intuition was religious and

aesthetic, affirming the universal order by exploring its beauty. Thus, in Tesauro's view, it is 'possible to say that poems are ugly or beautiful, but not that they are false or sophistic. The nature of *cavillazione retorica* tells us that one does not inquire into truth with literary statement, but simply states that which is to be enjoyed.'[19] Cowley did, in the first Book of the *Davideis*, propose the universal order as an object of aesthetic delight:

> Such was *Gods Poem*, this *Worlds* new *Essay*;
> So wild and rude in its first draught it lay;
> Th'ungovern'd parts no *Correspondence* knew,
> An artless *war* from thwarting *Motions* grew;
> Till they to *Number* and fixt Rules were brought
> By the *eternal Minds Poetique Thought*.   (P, 253)

But, as I have argued in Chapter 5, it was precisely the feeling that the poem ought to 'inquire into truth with literary statement' which created difficulties for Cowley. He solved the problem in 'The Muse' by identifying poetry with knowledge, and in doing so exceeded the limits of any established poetic, 'Metaphysical' or otherwise. His interests lay with a rather more systematic pursuit of knowledge than that provided by the aesthetic 'thrill' of 'Metaphysical' wit. The Spanish theorist Baltasar Gracián held that the different representations joined in metaphor constituted two 'knowable extremes', and that wit was the faculty capable of binding these extremes together, an attitude one might relate to Locke's distinction between two operations of the mind, 'sagacity' and 'illation':

> By the one, it finds out; and by the other, it so orders the inter-
> mediate *ideas* as to discover what connexion there is in each link
> of the chain whereby the extremes are held together, and there-
> by, as it were, to draw into view the truth sought for: which is
> what we call *illation* or *inference*, and consists in nothing but the
> perception of the connexion there is between the *ideas* in each
> step of the deduction, whereby the mind comes to see either the
> certain agreement or disagreement of any two *ideas*, as in dem-
> onstration, in which it arrives at knowledge, or their probable
> connexion on which it gives or withholds its assent, as in
> opinion.[20]

Sagacity, the perception of distant correspondences, is roughly equivalent to Gracián's notion of wit as the joining of 'knowable extremes', but Locke, like Hobbes, was primarily concerned with the inferential links of 'the chain whereby the extremes are held together', the contiguous relation of 'any two *ideas*'. 'The Muse', I think, identifies poetry not with 'sagacity' but with the techniques used by the natural philosopher to 'draw into view the truth sought for'. It works through a poetic of ornament and a poetic of correspondence, moving on to a definition of poetry as cognitive process, as that which enables one to know the identity of the momentary experiences of life. In this respect, one might contrast its mode of development with George Herbert's 'Vanitie (1)', a poem which includes images similar to those employed by Cowley in stanza 3 of 'The Muse': the astronomer threading the spheres with his 'quick-piercing minde'; the diver cutting the waves with his side; the 'subtil Chymick' stripping the creature naked, 'till he finde/The callow principles within their nest'.[21] Yet Herbert's point, of course, is that all such knowledge is a distracting vanity: 'What hath not man sought out and found,/But his deare God?'. The poem's development resolves a tension between false and true states of mind, revealing to Herbert the reality of his own nature. But the type of knowledge which Herbert considers a distraction is for Cowley a value in itself and 'The Muse', far from resolving any internal tension, develops open-endedly from idea to idea. There is a danger that my analysis may have exaggerated the rigour of the poem, but it seems clear to me that whereas Cowley had previously conceived the function of poetry in terms of the ceremonial role played by the poet, he now wants to establish what kind of proposition a poem is, and ends up virtually identifying poetry with 'propositional truth'.

The next ode in the collection—not, I think, by coincidence—offers an account of the intellectual achievement of Thomas Hobbes:

> Vast *Bodies* of *Philosophie*
>   I oft have seen, and read,
>   But all are *Bodies Dead*,
>   Or *Bodies* by *Art fashioned*;
> I never yet the *Living Soul* could see,
>   But in thy *Books* and *Thee*.
> 'Tis onely *God* can know

Whether the fair *Idea* thou dost show
Agree intirely with his *own* or no.
      This I dare boldly tell,
'Tis so *like Truth* 'twill serve our turn as well.
Just, as in *Nature* thy *Proportions* be,
As full of *Concord* their *Varietie*,
As *firm* the parts upon their *Center* rest,
And all so *Solid* are that they at least
As much as *Nature, Emptiness detest*.   (P, 188)

Hobbes was self-consciously an innovator, a man who regarded previous philosophies as not only false but meaningless, and he could not therefore be praised in traditional or ritual manner. Cowley argues that only God can know whether or not Hobbes's formulations correspond to the truth, and so each individual must make up his own mind about their probable accuracy. This argument is perfectly consonant with the emphasis placed by Cowley's Pindaric mode on the succession of thoughts in the individual mind, but where 'The Muse' had simulated imaginative flight by rapid variation of line-length, the last six lines of the stanza settle into a pentametric mould, stabilising the volatility of the Pindaric form. 'To Mr. Hobs' includes several such 'blocks' of regular rhythm which serve to establish the dignity and resonance of its statement.

But Cowley was virtually alone among his contemporaries in celebrating, without qualification, the scope of Hobbes's achievement, and he had therefore to provide a context for his praise, lifting it above the level of mere opinion or personal regard. Stanzas 2–4 provide this context, placing Hobbes's work within a mythology of 'intellectual revolution'. Stanza 2 is a kind of 'progress-piece', describing the progressive degeneration of philosophy since the time of Aristotle, and the dynamic of this movement is inertial and Pindaric, not related to the disclosure of any ultimate truth. Stanza 3 examines the consequences of this degeneration, while stanza 4, by comparing Hobbes to Columbus, establishes the appropriate modern context for his philosophy, since the discovery of new worlds was thought to have inaugurated an era of equivalent intellectual expansion. Bacon, for example, claimed that

   this proficience in navigation and discovery may plant also

great expectation of the further proficience and augmentation of the sciences; especially as it may seem that these two are ordained by God to be coevals, that is, to meet in one age. For so the Prophet Daniel, in speaking of the latter times, foretells 'That many shall go to and fro on the earth, and knowledge shall be increased', as if the opening and thorough passage of the world, and the increase of knowledge, were appointed to be in the same age . . .[22]

By employing the comparison with Columbus, Cowley was able to view Hobbes's philosophy as part of the intellectual effort of an age, giving his exposition an ideological as well as a personal frame of reference. But the myths of degeneration and expansion are themselves a product of that age, a new code of procedure established by the writing of the *Leviathan* or indeed 'To Mr. Hobs'. They do not by themselves guarantee the validity of those works which are referred to them; in that sense they might be considered provisional. Cowley has put one in a position to appreciate Hobbes's achievement, but he has not as yet defined the nature of this achievement, for Hobbes differs from Columbus in that he both discovered and colonised his 'learn'd *America*'.

Since the parameters of analysis and appreciation have not been established in advance, by a traditional code of procedure, Cowley has ultimately to rely on a personal assessment, and reverts in stanza 5 to a more subjective position:

> I little thought before,
> (Nor being my *own self* so *poor*
> Could comprehend so vast a *store*)
> That all the *Wardrobe* of rich *Eloquence*,
> Could have afforded half enuff,
> Of *bright*, of *new*, and *lasting* stuff,
> To cloath the mighty *Limbs* of thy *Gigantique Sence*.
> Thy solid *Reason* like the *shield* from heaven
> To the *Trojan Heroe* given,
> Too strong to take a mark from any mortal dart,
> Yet shines with *Gold* and *Gems* in every part,
> And *Wonders* on it grave'd by the learn'd hand of *Art*,
> A *shield* that gives delight
> Even to the *enemies* sight,
> Then when they're sure to *lose* the *Combat by't*.

The first sentence establishes a personal, rather than ideological, context for the understanding of Hobbes's philosophy; one notices the characteristic qualifying parenthesis. But a sense of personal inadequacy is hardly the most convincing of commendations, so Cowley, amplifying his praise of logical coherence in the first stanza, again fashions a heroic parallel, comparing Hobbes's intellect to the shield made for Aeneas by Vulcan. On this shield, as he remarks in a footnote, 'was graven all the *Roman History*', and the comparison reinforces his earlier statement that Hobbes had '*planted, peopled, built* and *civiliz'd*' a philosophical New World; Hobbes, clearly, has constructed, rather than discovered or revealed, an intellectual system. Vulcan was the god of fire, and therefore traditionally associated with artifice. 'It was well said by Democritus', Bacon wrote,

'That the truth of nature lies hid in certain deep mines and caves'. It was not ill said by the alchemists, 'That Vulcan is a second nature, and imitates that dexterously and compendiously which nature works circuitously and in length of time'. Why therefore should we not divide Natural Philosophy into two parts, the mine and the furnace; and make two professions or occupations of natural philosophers, some to be miners and some to be smiths? . . . The one searching into the bowels of nature, the other shaping nature as on an anvil.

Cowley certainly regarded the part of natural philosophy devoted to 'searching into the bowels of nature' as a necessary and worthwhile activity, and in stanza 3 he complained that

> We search among the *Dead*
> For Treasures *Buried*,
> Whilst still the *Liberal Earth* does hold
> So many *Virgin Mines* of *undiscover'ed Gold*.

Hobbes, however, could only be identified with artifice rather than observation, with the products of anvil and furnace. In the Introduction to *Leviathan*, he had written that nature,

the art whereby God hath made and governs the world, is by the *art* of man, as in many other things, so in this also imitated, that it can make an artificial animal. For seeing life is but a motion of limbs, the beginning whereof is in some principal part within; why may we not say, that all *automata* (engines that move themselves by springs and wheels as doth a watch) have an artificial life? . . . *Art* goes yet further, imitating that rational and most excellent work of nature, *man*. For by art is created that great LEVIATHAN called a COMMONWEALTH, or STATE, in Latin CIVITAS, which is but an artificial man; though of greater stature and strength than the natural, for whose protection and defence it was intended . . .[23]

Cowley praised Hobbes for constructing a 'body' of philosophy to replace barren speculation, and admired the 'mighty *Limbs*' of his '*Gigantique Sence*'. In Baconian terms, the *Leviathan* undeniably belonged to the category of the 'furnace': 'Vulcan is a second nature, and imitates that dexterously and compendiously which nature works circuitously and in length of time'. The artificer of the state, Hobbes had said, 'is *man*'. Stanza 5 goes a long way towards putting one in a position to understand the nature of Hobbes's philosophy, but it ends on a note of subjective awe, of impression rather than rational conviction—the shield 'gives delight/Even to the *enemies* sight'. The process of understanding is not yet complete.

In stanza 1, Cowley had described the logical coherence of Hobbes's thought, and the poem concludes by returning to Hobbes the man:

> Nor can the *Snow* which now cold *Age* does shed
> >   Upon thy reverend Head,
> Quench or allay the noble *Fires* within,
> >   But all which thou hast *bin*,
> >   And all that *Youth* can *be* thou'rt yet,
> >   So fully still dost Thou
> Enjoy the *Manhood*, and the *Bloom* of *Wit*,
> And all the *Natural Heat*, but not the *Feaver* too.
> So *Contraries* on *Aetna's* top conspire,
> Here hoary *Frosts*, and by them breaks out *Fire*.
> A secure *peace* the *faithful Neighbors* keep,
> Th'emboldned *Snow* next to the *Flame* does *sleep*.
> >   And if we weigh, like *Thee*,
> >   *Nature*, and *Causes*, we shall see
> >   That thus it *needs must be*,

> To things *Immortal Time* can do no wrong,
> And that which never is *to Dye*, for ever must be *Young*.

Cowley pointed out in a footnote that the 'Description of the Neighbourhood of *Fire* and *Snow* upon *Aetna* (but not the application of it) is imitated out of *Claud. L.* 1. *de Raptu Pros*', and he also referred the reader to Seneca's 79th Epistle. Seneca remarks that, although the topic is a 'matter of ritual for all poets', those who have used it 'seem to me not to have forestalled all that could be said, but merely to have opened the way'. The use of such a 'ritual' figure cannot be merely for witty effect. It must have some special 'application', and the attribution to Hobbes of 'noble *Fires* within' obviously continues his identification with Vulcan, artificer and god of fire. Cowley provided a lengthy footnote on the use Aeneas made of the shield given him by Venus, but he did not discuss another aspect of the Virgilian context, the manufacture of the shield (I give the Loeb translation, since we are concerned with the sense only):

> Hard by the Sicanian coast and Aeolian Lipare rises an island, steep with smoking rocks. Beneath it thunders a cave, and the vaults of Aetna, scooped out by Cyclopean forges; strong strokes are heard echoing groans from the anvils, masses of Chalyb steel hiss in the caverns, and the fire pants in the furnace—the home of Vulcan and the land Vulcan's by name. Hither in that hour the Lord of Fire came down from high heaven.[24]

Since Cowley had so carefully prepared the Virgilian context in the preceding stanza, it seems legitimate to suppose its relevance to the 'application' of the Aetna-figure. In which case, the noble fires inside Hobbes's snowy appearance can be identified with the anvil and furnace of Vulcan's laboratory. One poem in *The Mistress* had drawn a parallel between the establishment of Vulcan's shop inside Aetna and the discovery of Cupid's forge in the lover's breast:

> What *Mines* of *Sulphur* in my breast do ly,
> That feed th' eternal burnings of my heart?
> Not *Aetna* flames more fierce or constantly,
> The sounding shop of *Vulcans* smoaky art;

Vulcan his shop has placed there,
And *Cupids Forge* is set up here.   (P, 120)

In the later poem the forge is that of the intellect, and although the
rationality of Hobbes's work may be divine in provenance—
something, Cowley had said, we cannot know—its functions are
recognisably human. The figure involves a kind of artistic proof in
the sense that it draws on the traditional wisdom stored in the
Aeneid, but its purpose is to draw attention to the power of the *individual* mind, outside any divine or even social context. Cowley's
use of it is analytic, no 'matter of ritual'; he wants to persuade his
readers to think for themselves, as Hobbes had done ('if we weigh,
like *Thee/Nature*, and *Causes*'). The ode weaves in and out of ceremony, applying familiar ritualised tropes to a man whose great-
ness lay in his disregard of conventions, his ability to concentrate
on 'the proposition itself'. Pindarism, in short, made it possible to
meet Hobbes on his own ground; Cowley was almost alone among
his contemporaries in doing so.

IV

The *Pindarique Odes*, however, do not simply record the triumphant advance of human knowledge. The 'warlike, various, and
. . . tragical age' enters into them as deeply as it had into *The Civil
War* and the *Davideis*, and they constitute a no less bitter and
perplexed statement of Cowley's situation. 'Destinie', the ode
which succeeds 'To Mr. Hobs', argues in the most pessimistic
terms that free will is an illusion, and it has an appropriate epi-
graph from Manilius—

    Hoc quoque fatale est sic ipsum expendere fatum

—which, as translated by Thomas Creech, reads:

    'Tis *Fate* that we should thus dispute of *Fate*.[25]

The statement that human thought cannot avoid fatalism contrasts strangely with the confidence shown by the two previous
odes in the ability of poetry to extend the empire of human
knowledge. But it is a contrast manifest not only in

the *Pindarique Odes* but also in Manilius's *Astronomica*, Book IV of which provides the epigraphs for 'Destinie' and 'Life'. On one hand, the *Astronomica* strongly identifies poetry with the pursuit of scientific knowledge, and the invocations at the beginning of each Book describe, in terms very similar to 'The Muse', the flight of Manilius's muse to the skies, where it will discover the secrets of nature. When Sir Edward Sherburne translated Book I in 1675, he obviously regarded it as propaganda for the cause of science, and appended a long list of the most famous astronomers, ancient and modern; Cowley himself, in his *Proposition for the Advancement of Experimental Philosophy*, included Manilius among the Latin poets whose work was to be recommended because it treated of 'Natural Matters'. But the purpose of the *Astronomica* was to prove the influence of the stars on men's lives, and Manilius thus demonstrates not only the intellectual power and freedom of the human mind, but also its ultimate helplessness and subjection to fate. Cowley's *Odes* follow this oscillating pattern exactly, veering between the forceful optimism of 'The Muse' or 'To Mr. Hobs' and a bitter fatalism, Cowley's own position lying not so much at one or other extreme as in the oscillation itself, the feeling that the two attitudes, although contradictory, were equally valid. In this sense, the *Astronomica*, a relatively obscure poem, can be said to have exerted as powerful an influence on the shape of the *Odes* as anything Pindar wrote.

The 'double madnes' of impossible alternatives is a theme which has cropped up several times during the course of this study. I would risk the generalisation that a society which found it increasingly difficult to operate traditional codes had become vulnerable to violent fluctuations between a new confidence in the power of the human mind and a renewed sense of human fallibility. The lack of 'support' from the placing structures of cultural tradition, in other words, could be liberating; or it could be rather frightening. One might consider in this respect the fourth of Descartes' *Meditations on First Philosophy*. Descartes begins the meditation by observing how in the past few days he has been able to examine the workings of his own mind in isolation from any context. By acknowledging that he doubts and is therefore an 'incomplete and dependent being', he is led to conceive the idea of a 'complete and independent' being (God) with absolute clarity and certainty. Assurance thus arises out of the awareness of fallibility, persuading Descartes that he has discovered a 'road' from the contemplation of the true God to the knowledge of the other objects of the universe. This knowledge must be valid, because God could not possibly wish to deceive, and Descartes concludes that his reason will not lead him astray if used properly; as long as he directs his mind wholly towards God he can discover in himself no cause of error or falsity. Immediately afterwards, however, when returning from the thought of God to the thought of himself, experience forces him to recognise his own fallibility and the ease with which he deceives himself. He has not only a positive idea of supreme perfection, but also a negative idea of nothing—a complete removal from perfection—and he himself is 'intermediate' between the two. Rather, as the structure of the *Meditation* shows, he is condemned to a perpetual oscillation between the two extremes. Similarly, 'The Muse' and 'To Mr. Hobs' place the reader on an '*open Road*' to the knowledge of natural matters, while 'Life and Fame' asserts that life itself is founded on nothing and that thought and language are mere vanity. I do not imagine that Cowley had ever read, or at least absorbed, the Cartesian philosophy, but it seems to me that he faced a dilemma experienced by some of his most intelligent and radical contemporaries.

'Destinie' represents an emphatic and consciously disruptive swing back towards the feeling of helplessness. It describes an imaginary game of chess where the pieces have apparent autonomy of movement, and the first stanza professes admiration of such anthropomorphic initiative and verve:

> Lo, the unbred, ill-organ'd *Pieces* prove,
>   As full of *Art*, and *Industrie*,
>   Of *Courage* and of *Policie*
> As *we our selves* who think there's nothing *Wise* but *We*.
>
> (P, 192)

But it turns out that the pieces are being moved by angels, and this provokes from Cowley a far more fatalistic reflection:

> With *Man*, alas, no otherwise it proves,
>   An *unseen Hand* makes all their *Moves*.
>   And some are *Great*, and some are *Small*,
> Some climb to *good*, some from *good Fortune* fall,
>   Some *Wisemen*, and some *Fools* we call,
> *Figures*, alas, of *Speech*, for *Desti'ny plays us all*.

The terms used earlier—art, industry, courage, policy—are meaningless figures of speech, denoting factors which play no real part in human destiny. Even the Pindaric flexibility of rhyme has been reduced to a fatalism (small, fall, call, all); life has a single termination, a single note. Such despair has also a political context, and in his description of the chess-game Cowley admires the 'proud *Pawn*' advancing down the board until it becomes another '*Thing* and *Name*', and criticises the 'false *Moves*' of the 'losing party' and the '*ill Conduct*' of the '*Mated King*'. But he is primarily concerned with his own destiny, and one feels here the influence of the *Astronomica*, with its insistence on man's subjection to fate:

> Vain Man forbear, of Cares, unload thy Mind,
> Forget thy Hopes, and give thy Fears to Wind;
> For *Fate* rules all, its stubborn Laws must sway
> The lower World, and *Man* confin'd obey.
> *As we are Born we Dye, our Lots are cast,*
> *And our first Hour disposeth of our last.*
> Then as the influence of the Stars ordains,
> To Empires *Kings* are doom'd, and *Slaves* to Chains.[26]

Book IV then explains how each star is the sign of a particular career, allocating a destiny to each individual: soldiering, civil employment, law, marriage, wealth through commerce, etc. Cowley is in no doubt as to his own fate: 'Me from the *womb* the *Midwife Muse* did take'. The demonstration of freedom, initiative and power in the first two odes has been superseded by a sense of fixity and helplessness—

> With *Fate* what boots it to contend?
> Such I *began*, such *am*, and so must *end*

—Cowley can now offer only defiance:

> No Matter, *Cowley*, let proud *Fortune* see,
> That *thou* canst *her* despise no less then *she* does *Thee*.
>   Let all her gifts the portion be
>   Of Folly, Lust, and Flattery,
>   Fraud, Extortion, Calumnie,
>   Murder, Infidelitie,
>   Rebellion and Hypocrisie.

The catalogue has a flatness of rhythm and rhyme which again almost parodies the closeness of the Pindaric mode to prose argument or to 'discursion'; for significant features of the Pindaric mode, such as monotony of rhyme or variability of metre, reflect with equal facility both of Cowley's positions and thus serve to emphasise the oscillation which structures the *Odes*.

The next six odes ('Brutus', 'To Dr. Scarborough', 'Life and Fame', 'The Extasie', 'To the New Year', 'Life') simply extend the oscillating series further, veering both in subject-matter and in tone from one extreme to the other. They have their peaks of optimism, sometimes in the celebration of human abilities (Scarborough's successful treatment of plague) but more often in pious contemplation. 'The Extasie', for example, has the appearance of an interpolation, since its form is virtually regular, and Cowley may well have intended to set it against the fatalism of its predecessor, 'Life and Fame'. It describes the process of self-transcendence in thoroughly conventional terms, recalling Donne's account in 'The Second Anniversary' of the 'extasie' of the soul's flight, or the numerous invitations to ecstasy in Benlowes's *Theophila*. '*Divine Poesie*', Benlowes wrote in the Preface to *Theophila*, 'is the internal Triumph of the Mind, rapt with S. *Paul* into the third Heaven, where She contemplates Ineffables', a state Cowley reaches by stanza 6. 'Life' attempts to transform self-contempt into a *contemptus mundi* which again recalls 'The Second Anniversary'. 'This to thy soule allow', Donne had written, contemplating a pious death,

> Thinke thy shell broke, thinke thy Soule hatch'd but now.
> And thinke this slow-pac'd soule, which late did cleave
> To'a body, and went but by the bodies leave,
> Twenty, perchance, or thirty mile a day,
> Dispatches in a minute all the way
> Twixt heaven, and earth . . .[27]

Cowley echoes this sense of welcome release from the constraints of body, but with a significant difference of emphasis:

> The ripened *Soul* longs from his pris'on to come,
> But we would *seal*, and *sow* up, if we could, the *Womb*.
> We seek to close and plaster up by Art

> The *cracks* and *breaches* of the' extended *Shell*,
>> And in that narrow *Cell*
>> Would rudely force to dwell,
> The noble vigorours *Bird* already *wing'd* to part. (P, 210)

Whereas Donne had been, explicitly and by the supple rhythm of the verse, forward-looking, thinking past a worldly frame of reference, Cowley reveals a greater preoccupation with human perversity than with the process of faith. The imprisoning triple rhyme outweighs the compensating strength and poise of the last line. Indeed, throughout the poem Cowley seems morbidly obsessed with human vanity; the semantic sonority of the terms men use to assert the value of life—*Nobilitie, Herauldrie, Posteritie*—is cruelly reduced by the failed sonority of another triple rhyme. Troughs of depression succeed each optimistic peak with such bleak intensity that Richard Hurd, Cowley's eighteenth-century editor, glossed a line in 'Life and Fame' with a reference to Pascal's *Pensées*.[28]

V

None of these poems remotely compares with 'The Muse' or 'To Mr. Hobs', and their unflattering view of human nature smothers the confidence which had appeared to animate the Pindaric experiment. The two remaining odes, 'The 34. Chapter of the Prophet Isaiah' and 'The Plagues of Egypt', attempt to check this unregulated veering between extremes by adopting the position of prophecy:

> Awake, and with attention hear,
>> Thou *drowsie World*, for it concerns thee near;
>> Awake, I say, and listen well,
> To what from *God*, I, his *loud Prophet*, tell.　　　　(P, 211)

There are echoes of the tone of *The Mistress*, but this time the assertiveness is more sustained. Prophecy must be optimistic to the extent that it predicts the advent of a saviour, and pessimistic to the extent that it laments the unpreparedness of contemporary society for such an occurrence. Which is all very well in theory but not in practice: both odes are dreadful at some length. Their interest lies in the light they throw on the theory rather than the practice of Pindaric style, and 'The 34. Chapter' includes, in a footnote, a passage which has become the crux of modern interpretations of Cowley's Pindarism. I shall quote the passage in full, because it has too often been distorted by selection:

> The manner of the *Prophets* writing, especially of *Isaiah*, seems to me very like that of *Pindar*; they pass from one thing to another with almost *Invisible connexions*, and are full of words and expressions of the highest and boldest flights of *Poetry*, as may be seen in this Chapter, where there are as extraordinary Figures as can be found in any *Poet* whatsoever; and the connexion is so difficult, that I am forced to adde a little, and leave out a great deal to make it seem *Sense* to us, who are not used to that elevated way of expression. The *Commentators* differ, and some would have it to be a *Prediction* of the destruction of *Judaea*, as *Hugo, Lyran*, and others; the rest understand it as a *Prophesie* of the Day of *Judgment*. The design of it to me seems to be this, first to denounce great desolations and ruines to *all Countrys*, and then to do it more particularly to *Judaea*, as which was to suffer a greater measure of them than the rest of the world; as it has done, I think, much more than any other Land under the Sun; and to illustrate these confusions by the similitude of them to those of the last Day, though in the Text there be no Transition from the *subject* to the *similitude*; for the old fashion of writing, was like *Disputing* in *Enthymemes*, where half is left out to be supplyed by the Hearer: ours is like *Syllogisms*, where all that is meant is exprest. (P, 214)

Paul Korshin claims that when Cowley refers to 'the old fashion of writing' he is 'probably analogizing methods cultivated by the Hebrew poets to those presently favored by the English Metaphysicals'; and that '*Invisible connexions*' may 'refer as well to the chief mode of Metaphysical wit, *discordia concors*'.[29] This interpretation implies that the passage should be regarded as a general statement about poetics. But the footnote is explicitly concerned with the structural organisation of Chapter 34 of Isaiah. Although it does begin with a comparison between the 'manner of the *Prophets* writing' and 'that of *Pindar*', the problem of difficult connections is then related specifically to Cowley's attempt to make sense out of one chapter of Isaiah. Some commentators, he says, think that the

chapter predicts the destruction of Judaea, others that it is a prophecy of the day of judgment. According to Cowley, it combines
three aims: to pronounce doom on the world, and on Judaea; and
'to illustrate these confusions by the similitude of them to those of
the last Day'. The difficulty of connection is not between vehicle
and tenor in any number of figures but between the parts of the
argument, which Cowley has just outlined. He introduces the distinction between an enthymemic and a syllogistic mode of argument in order to illustrate the specific problem, not as an analogy
with methods 'presently favored' by the Metaphysicals. 'The
name of PROPHET', Hobbes had written, 'signifieth in Scripture
. . . sometimes one that speaketh incoherently, as men that are
distracted'. Incoherent speech 'was amongst the Gentiles taken
for one sort of prophecy, because the prophets of their oracles,
intoxicated with a spirit or vapour from the cave of the Pythian
oracle at Delphi, were for the time really mad, and spake like
madmen'. Furthermore, as St Paul recognised, 'the poets of the
heathen, that composed hymns and other sorts of poems in the
honour of their gods, were called *vates*, prophets'.[30] Cowley, like
Hobbes, was interested in prophecy as a mode of discourse, and
he too made the comparison with a heathen poet on that basis. His
discussion does have a general relevance but, because it is firmly
based on the analysis of the 34th Chapter of Isaiah, it develops a
theory of discourse rather than of poetry, and for that reason analogies with a Metaphysical poetic of correspondence seem to me
inappropriate. I think one might instead compare the footnote
with Hobbes's concept of discursion. Both men suggest that there
are two modes of discourse, casual and orderly, enthymemic and
syllogistic; both attempt to replace, systematically, disorder by
order. Hobbes found that neither the human mind nor human
society revealed any principle of order, and he therefore sought to
impose on both the discipline of method. Cowley's 'The 34. Chapter of the Prophet Isaiah' replaced the disorder of the biblical text,
with its obscure connections, by a more methodical version.

The *Pindarique Odes* represent a notable attempt to do justice to
contemporary preoccupation with the workings of the individual
mind. Cowley continued to write Pindaric odes after the Restoration, but he was then moving in a different intellectual milieu. As
the friend of Sprat and Evelyn, and the author of the *Proposition for
the Advancement of Experimental Philosophy*, he was the poet most
closely associated with the Royal Society. One of the Restoration

'Men of Wit and Sense', Daniel Fleming, purchased, between December 1667 and January 1669, two books by Sprat, two by Glanvill, one by Boyle, and one by Wilkins, as well as several numbers of the *Philosophical Transactions*. During that period he apparently bought only one book of poems, Cowley's *Works*, on 24 July 1668. Cowley also became intimate with Martin Clifford, whose advocacy of human reason sparked off a controversy. Dame Sarah Cowper wrote in her diary of Clifford's 'great Veneration for Bp Wilkins Dr Tillot: Dr Barrow and the like', the theological group which had the closest connections with the development of science.[31] There are enough similarities between Cowley's Pindarism and Restoration formulations of scientific method for one to suggest that they were in some sense answering a common need or preoccupation. Theorists such as Boyle and Glanvill emphasised above all the importance of suspending judgment, so that one's results would not be predetermined by assumptions or *a priori* criteria. Similarly, the Pindaric ode did not, in theory, develop according to any external prescription or reveal any preconceived pattern. 'The true *Experimenting*', Sprat wrote,

has this one thing inseparable from it, never to be a *fix'd* and *settled Art*, and never to be *limited* by constant Rules. This, perhaps, may be shewn too in other *Arts*; as in that of *Invention*, of which, though in *Logick* and *Rhetorick*, so many bounds, and helps are given: yet I believe very few have argued or discoursed by those *Topicks*. But whether that be unconfin'd, or no, it is certain, that Experimenting is . . .[32]

Sprat's willingness to generalise from experiment to invention, from a mode of knowledge to a mode of argument, is interesting, and his disregard of the principle of decorum recalls his earlier statement that Pindaric style is unconfined as to subject-matter. The aim of Cowley's odes was precisely 'never to be a *fix'd* and *settled Art*, and never to be *limited* by constant Rules'. So there was perhaps some substance to Meric Casaubon's accusation that Sprat had encouraged a poetry based on experiment rather than on classical mythology. Cowley's later odes certainly sustain his interest in Pindarism as a mode of knowledge and argument rather than as lyric expression, but the very direction of this interest ran counter to the long tradition of irregular verse. 'Since Pindar was the prince of lyric poets', Dryden wrote in the Preface to *Sylvae* (1685),

> let me have leave to say that, in imitating him, our numbers should for the most part be lyrical. For variety, or rather where the majesty of thought requires it, they may be stretched to the English heroic of five feet, and to the French Alexandrine of six. But the ear must preside, and direct the judgment to the choice of numbers: without the nicety of this the harmony of Pindaric verse can never be complete; the cadency of one line must be a rule to that of the next; and the sound of the former must slide gently into that which follows, without leaping from one extreme into another. It must be done like the shadowings of a picture, which fall by degrees into a darker colour.[33]

Cowley undoubtedly exceeded the alexandrine—some of his lines have as many as eight feet—and his rhyming of a two-syllable line with an alexandrine in 'The Muse' hardly manifested a great concern for subtle gradations. Any proceeding 'by degrees', in sound or sense, would also contradict the principle of hardiness. But the difference is a more fundamental one. Dryden said that the ear should preside over the judgment in the choice of numbers; Cowley, if my analysis of the Odes is correct, thought the opposite. Dryden's Pindarics, following his own prescriptions, formed part of the development of the irregular ode from Milton to Wordsworth, Coleridge and Shelley, whereas Cowley's represent a brave attempt to keep pace with 'intellectual revolution'.

References

Books and articles listed in the bibliography are cited here by their short titles only.

1 INTRODUCTION

1. See the studies listed in the bibliography under Coltman, Hill (1958, 1977), Langley, Rivers and Wallace.
2. See, inter alia, the studies listed in the bibliography under Donahue, Fussner, Hoopes, Jones, Koyré, Popkin, Spragens, Trotter (Chapter 1), Van Leeuwen and Webster.
3. *English Works*, IV, p. 28; II, pp. 303–5; *Leviathan*, Oakeshott (ed.), p. 42.
4. My understanding of the term 'locutionary' does not derive from the more precise sense given it by J. L. Austin, who distinguished between 'locutionary', 'illocutionary' and 'perlocutionary' acts: *How to Do Things with Words* (Oxford, 1962).

2 CIVIL WAR

1. *The Civil War*, Book I, lines 1–2. References will henceforth be incorporated into the text, giving Book and line numbers.
2. Lines 187–9 in the 1642 edition: O Hehir, *Expans'd Hieroglyphicks*, p. 122.
3. *The Civil War*, p. 37; an obvious point, but the obviousness (the sheer familiarity of the epic pattern) *is* the point.

3 THE LYRICS

1. Walsh, Preface to *Letters and Poems, Amorous and Gallant* (1692) Sig A3 recto; Dryden, *Of Dramatic Poesy*, II, p. 76; Oldmixon, *Arts of Logick and Rhetorick*, p. 333.
2. *The School of Love*, pp. 97, 118.
3. Sidney, *Poems*, pp. 60–1; Henry Constable, *Diana*, in *Poems*, p. 214; Sidney, *Poems*, p. 187.
4. Daniel, *Poems*, p. 15.
5. Quotation from L. A. Beaurline, 'Dudley North's Criticism of Metaphysical

Poetry', pp. 305–8.

6. Leishman, *The Monarch of Wit*, p. 154; Kermode, *Renaissance Essays*, p. 121.

7. S. T. Coleridge, characterisation of Donne's wit in marginal notes on the *Songs and Sonets, Coleridge on The Seventeenth Century*, R. F. Brinkley (ed.), pp. 522, 526.

8. *The School of Love*, p. 223. It might be argued that the less 'orthodox' terms of description employed throughout this chapter are reductively neutral, even mechanistic. When these terms are used, however, their aim is to describe how literary practice becomes convention, not how individual readers respond to individual lyrics.

9. *Minor Poems*, p. 424.

10. *Poems*, I, p. 55.

11. Cleveland, *Poems*, pp. 18, 59; Rochester, *Complete Poems*, pp. 90, 51. Hobbes, *English Works*, III, p. 15, source noted by J. Treglown, 'The Satirical Inversion of Some English Sources in Rochester's Poetry', RES, n.s. 24 (1973) p. 44.

12. *Steps*, pp. 153–5.

13. Watzlawick, Beavin and Jackson, *Pragmatics of Human Communication*, pp. 212–13; see also Bateson, *Steps*, passim.

14. Ibid., p. 217.

15. Stubbe, *A Censure upon Certaine Passages Contained in the History of the Royal Society* (Oxford, 1670) p. 62; Elys, *An Exclamation . . . Against an Apology . . . for Mr. Cowley's Lascivious and Prophane Verses* (1670), p. 5.

16. Addison, *Spectator*, 62, Bond (ed.), I, p. 265; *Miscellaneous Works*, A. C. Guthkelch (ed.), 2 volumes (1914) I, p. 144; *Spectator*, I, p. 266. Tuve, *Elizabethan and Metaphysical Imagery*, especially Chapter 10.

17. Freud, *Complete Psychological Works*, J. Strachey (ed.), 24 volumes (1953–) 14, p. 186; Von Domarus, 'Specific Laws of Logic in Schizophrenia', in *Language and Thought in Schizophrenia*, J. S. Kasanin (ed.) (Berkeley, 1944) pp. 104–14; Bateson, *Steps*, p. 177; Kurt Goldstein, 'Methodological Approach to the Study of Schizophrenic Thought Disorder', in Kasanin, p. 34.

18. *Poems and Dramas*, I, p. 104.

19. *Steps*, p. 181.

20. *The Art of Love*, Loeb edition, I, lines 615–6 and 653–6, pp. 54, 56. The second passage reads: 'Phalaris too roasted in his fierce bull the limbs of Perillus; its maker first made trial of his ill-omened work . . . for there is no juster law than that contrivers of death should perish by their own contrivances'.

21. *Arts of Logick and Rhetorick*, p. 332.

22. *Heroides and Amores*, Loeb edition, p. 404: 'And look now, a fresh charge! Cypassis, the deft girl that tires your hair, is cast at me, accused of wronging her mistress' couch. Ye gods grant me better, if I have a mind to sin, than find my pleasure in a love of mean and despised lot! What man that is free would willingly mate with a slave, and clasp a waist that was cut with the lash? Add that her work is to dress your hair, and she pleases you with the ministry of her cunning hand; of course I would tamper with a servant so faithful to you!'; and ibid.: 'Perfect in setting hair aright in a thousand ways, but worthy to dress only that of goddesses, Cypassis, you whom I have found in our stolen delight not wholly simple, apt for your mistress' service, but more apt for mine—who is the tattler has told of our coming together'.

23. *Idler* 77, *Works*, W. J. Bate and others (ed.), III (New Haven, 1963) p. 239.
24. Cf. also another lyric much concerned with a mediating term, 'Bathing in the River', which echoes the rhetoric of Waller's 'Goe lovely Rose' (itself a marvellously adroit lyric of mediated address).

4   COWLEY AND CRASHAW

1. *Themis* (1963) p. 328.
2. *Complete Poetry*, p. 494.
3. H. Trevor-Roper, *Archbishop Laud*, pp. 357–8.
4. Warren, *Richard Crashaw*, p. 89; M. E. Rickey, *Rhyme and Meaning in Richard Crashaw* (Lexington, 1961).
5. Trevor-Roper, *Archbishop Laud*, p. 435; Laud, *Works*, I, pp. 28–9 and III, p. 155.
6. Cosin, *Works*, V, passim, and IV, pp. 241–318, respectively; *A Collection of Private Devotions*, pp. 13–4; *Works*, I, pp. 161, 162, 180 and 180–1.
7. A. L. Maycock, *Nicholas Ferrar of Little Gidding* (1938) p. 281.
8. *Archbishop Laud*, p. 137.
9. *Five Pious and Learned Discourses*, pp. 17, 23–4, 26, 28, and 41.
10. Quoted by Allen Pritchard, 'Puritan Charges Against Crashaw and Beaumont', p. 578. Crashaw translated two hymns by Aquinas.
11 Hagstrum, *The Sister Arts* (Chicago, 1958) p. 97; Beaumont, *Minor Poems*, p. 290; Carre, in Crashaw, *Complete Poetry*, p. 652.
12. *Richard Crashaw*, p. 221; *Poems of Richard Crashaw*, L. C. Martin (ed.), second edition (Oxford, 1957) p. xxxix.
13. *Psyche* (1648) p. 48; *Psyche* (1702) p. 46. For Herbert's influence on Crashaw, see H. Swanston, 'The Second "Temple"', *Durham University Journal*, 56 (1963) pp. 14–22.
14. *Psyche* (1648), p. 48.
15. R. R. Reuther, *Gregory of Nazianzanus*, p. 7; Jean Le Clerc, *The Lives of Clemens Alexandrinus, Eusebius . . . Gregory Nazianzen, and Prudentius* (1696) p. 188.
16. *Minor Poems*, pp. 271 and 267.
17. Le Clerc, *Lives*, p. 271; *Richard Crashaw*, p. 89; Le Clerc, *Lives*, pp. 228 and 188.
18. Shelford, *Discourses*, pp. 107, 42, 101, 115 and 114; Hooker, *Ecclesiastical Polity*, I, vii, 2, in *Works*, I, p. 220.
19. See Louis Martz, *The Poetry of Meditation*, Appendix 1.
20. M. F. Bertonasco, *Crashaw and the Baroque* (Alabama, 1971) pp. 67–9.
21. *Complete Poetry*, pp. 54, 26.
22. *Discourses*, p. 101.
23. *Complete Poetry*, pp. 146, 148.
24. On the order of stanzas in this poem, see Clarence Miller, 'The Order of Stanzas in Cowley and Crashaw's "On Hope"', SP, 61 (1964) pp. 64–73; and, more convincingly, G. W. Williams, 'The Order of Stanzas in Cowley and Crashaw's "On Hope"', SB, 22 (1969) pp. 207–10. I shall quote from the text printed in Crashaw's *Complete Poetry*.
25. 'The White Stone: Or, A Learned and Choice Treatise of Assurance', published with *An Elegant and Learned Discourse of the Light of Nature* (1652) pp. 107–8.

26. *Complete Poetry*, p. 71.

27. Ibid., pp. 34–5.

28. As, for example, in Beaumont's poem 'Hope'.

29. *Complete Poetry*, p. 149, lines 39–44.

30. Ibid., p. 150 and p. 149; Wood, cited in *Poems of Richard Crashaw*, Martin (ed.), p. 417.

31. A. F. Allison, 'Some Influences in Crashaw's Poem "On a Prayer Booke Sent to Mrs. M. R."', RES, 23 (1947) pp. 34–42.

32. It was a popular theme in seventeenth-century funeral orations. See, for example, Simon Patrick's sermon preached at the funeral of John Smith, printed in Smith's *Select Discourses* (1660).

5   THE SACRED POEM

1. 'The Date of Cowley's *Davideis*', p. 158.

2. *Muse's Hannibal*, pp. 153–4.

3. *Judah's Return to their Allegiance, and David's Return to his Crown and Kingdom* (1660) p. 1; cited by R. F. Jones, 'The Originality of *Absalom and Achitophel*', MLN, 46 (1931) pp. 211–8.

4. Cf. J. A. Mazzeo, 'Cromwell as Davidic King', in *Renaissance and Seventeenth-Century Studies*.

5. *Majestas Intemerata* (1649) p. 94. I owe the reference to T. R. Langley.

6. James I, *The True Law of free Monarchies* (Edinburgh, 1598) Sigs B5 recto, B7 verso, B7 verso—B8 recto; Cook, *King Charles, His Case* (1649), in *The Trial of King Charles the First*, J. G. Muddiman (ed.) (Edinburgh, n.d.) p. 236; Filmer, *Patriarcha and Other Political Writings*, p. 97; Hobbes, *Leviathan*, Oakeshott (ed.), p. 134.

7. *Complete Prose Works*, III, pp. 202–3, 212, 206.

8. 'Time, History and Eschatology in the Thought of Thomas Hobbes', p. 171.

9. *Leviathan*, pp. 312, 314, 78–9, 269.

10. 'Time, History and Eschatology', p. 173.

11. *Speeches*, W. C. Abott (ed.), 4 volumes (Cambridge, Mass., 1937–47) III, p. 589.

12. 1655 edition, O Hehir, p. 160.

13. J. M. Steadman, *Milton and the Renaissance Hero*, p. vi.

14. One of Humphrey Moseley's catalogues, bound in with an edition of Waller's *Poems* (1645), describes a Latin version of the *Davideis* as forthcoming. It never appeared.

15. *Lives*, I, p. 54.

16. Aristotle, *Rhetoric;* Ramus, *Dialectique;* cited by W. S. Howell, *Logic and Rhetoric in England*, pp. 68, 155–6.

17. Howell, ibid., pp. 375, 376; Hill, *Society and Puritanism*, p. 404.

18. See above, pp. 00.

19. C. A. Patrides, 'The Renaissance View of Time: A Bibliographical Note', NQ, 208 (1963) pp. 408–10.

20. Hobbes, *Of Liberty and Necessity, English Works*, IV, p. 270 (see also ibid., pp. 298–300 and Bramhall, *Works*, 5 volumes [Oxford, 1842–5] IV, pp. 523–4); Pocock, 'Time, History and Eschatology', pp. 174, 178; Milton,

Christian Doctrine, Complete Prose Works, VI, pp. 313–14; *Paradise Lost*, V, lines 580–3, *Works*, II, i, p. 164.

6   THE PINDARIC ODES

1. Sprat, *Life*, Sig B verso; Nethercot, *Muse's Hannibal*, p. 135.
2. *Works*, VIII, pp. 245–6.
3. Blondel, *Comparison*, p. 66; Kennett, *Lives and Characters*, p. 80.
4. 'Anglorum Pindarus', especially p. 302.
5. Dionysius, *On Literary Composition*, trans. W. Rhys Roberts (1910) p. 213; Dryden, *Of Dramatic Poesy*, I, p. 271.
6. Scott Elledge, 'Cowley's Ode "Of Wit" ', p. 186.
7. Monk, *The Sublime*, pp. 15–7.
8. *Spectator*, Bond (ed.), II, p. 128, IV, pp. 190–1, 189.
9. *On the Sublime*, Loeb edition, p. 127.
10. Hobbes, *English Works*, IV, pp. 14, 19; Manningham, *Two Discourses* (1681) p. 54.
11. *Greek Lyric Poetry*, pp. 11, 13, 6.
12. H. L. Tracy, 'Thought-Sequence in the Ode'.
13. *English Works*, III, p. 51.
14. *English Ode to 1660*, p. 133.
15. Hobbes, in Spingarn, II, p. 59; Benlowes, *Theophila* (1656) Sig A6 verso; *On the Sublime*, p. 225.
16. Mazzeo, *Renaissance and Seventeenth-Century Studies*, pp. 53, 54; Bacon, *Works*, IV, p. 292 (see also Sidney, 'Apologie', in Gregory Smith, I, p. 156); Benlowes, *Theophila*, p. 127 (the poem was begun in 1646, as shown by Harold Jenkins, *Edward Benlowes* [1952] p. 156).
17. *Works*, IV, pp. 305, 355.
18. Ibid., IV, p. 392.
19. *Renaissance and Seventeenth-Century Studies*, pp. 59, 50; Bethell, 'Gracián, Tesauro, and the Nature of Seventeenth-Century Wit'.
20. *Essay*, II, p. 262.
21. *Works*, p. 85. See also Milton, 'At a Vacation Exercise', *Works*, I, i, pp. 19–21.
22. Bacon, *Works*, IV, pp. 311–2. On Columbus and the glorification of science, see Steadman, 'Beyond Hercules: Bacon and the Scientist as Hero'.
23. Bacon, *Works*, Ibid., IV, p. 343 (see also p. 287); Hobbes, *Leviathan*, p. 5.
24. Seneca, *Epistulae Morales*, Loeb edition, II, p. 203; *Aeneid*, VIII, lines 416–23.
25. *The Five Books of M. Manilius*, Part II, p. 9.
26. Ibid., Part II, p. 4.
27. Benlowes, *Theophila*, Sig A6 recto; Donne, *Poems*, I, p. 256.
28. *Select Works of Mr. A. Cowley*, I, p. 177.
29. *From Concord to Dissent*, p. 17.
30. *English Works*, III, pp. 412, 414–5, 413.
31. For Fleming, see *The Flemings in Oxford*, J. R. Magrath (ed.), 3 volumes (Oxford, 1904–24) I, pp. 392–507; for Clifford, Harth, *Contexts of Dryden's Thought*, pp. 235–44; for Dame Cowper, Pritchard, 'Six Letters by Cowley', p. 256.
32. *History of the Royal Society*, p. 89.
33. *Of Dramatic Poesy*, II, pp. 32–3.

Bibliography

a) COWLEY

Poems (1656)
Works (1668)
Works, 3 volumes (1707–8). Volumes 1 and 2, tenth edition; volume 3, eighth edition
Select Works, R. Hurd (ed.), 2 volumes (1772)
English Writings, A. R. Waller (ed.), 2 volumes (Cambridge, 1905–6)
The Essays and Other Prose Writings, A. B. Gough (ed.) (Oxford, 1915)
The Mistress With Other Select Poems, J. Sparrow (ed.) (1926)
The Civil War, A. Pritchard (ed.) (Toronto, 1973)

b) PRIMARY SOURCES

Addison, J., R. Steele, and others. *The Spectator*, D. F. Bond (ed.), 5 volumes (Oxford, 1965)
Bacon, F., *Works*, (ed.) J. Spedding, R. L. Ellis, D. D. Heath, 14 volumes (1857–74)
Baker, T., *Reflections upon Learning* (1700)
Bayle, P., *Historical and Critical Dictionary: Selections*, trans. R. H. Popkin and C. Brush (Indianapolis, 1965)
Beaumont, J., *Psyche, or Loves Mysterie* (1648)
——*Psyche*, second edition (Cambridge, 1702)
——*Minor Poems*, E. Robinson (ed.) (1914)
Benlowes, E., *Sphinx Theologica, sive Musica Templi, ubi Discordia Concors* (Cambridge, 1636)
——*Theophila, or Love's Sacrifice* (1656)
Blondel, F., *The Comparison of Pindar and Horace*, trans. E. Sherburne (1696)

Boyle, R., *Certain Physiological Essays* (1661)

——*Some Considerations touching the Style of the H. Scriptures* (1661)

——*Some Considerations touching the Usefulnesse of Experimental Natural Philosophy*, second edition, 2 volumes (Oxford, 1664–71)

——*A Discourse of Things Above Reason* (1681)

——*The Sceptical Chymist*, Everyman's Library (1911)

Cary, L., Viscount Falkland, *Discourse of Infallibility*, T. Triplet (ed.) (1651)

Casaubon, M., *A Letter . . . to Peter du Moulin . . . Concerning Natural Experimental Philosophie* (Cambridge, 1669)

Charron, P., *Of Wisedome*, trans. S. Lennard (1651)

Chillingworth, W., *Works* (1704)

Cleveland, J., *Poems*, B. Morris and E. Withington (eds.) (Oxford, 1967)

Clifford, M., *A Treatise of Humane Reason* (1674)

Constable, H., *Poems*, J. Grundy (ed.) (Liverpool, 1960)

Cosin, J., *Works*, 5 volumes (Oxford, 1843–55)

——*A Collection of Private Devotions*, P. G. Stanwood (ed.) (Oxford, 1967)

Crashaw, R., *Complete Poetry*, G. W. Williams (ed.) (New York, 1972)

Culverwel, N., *An Elegant and Learned Discourse of the Light of Nature* (1652)

Daniel, S., *Poems and A Defence of Rhyme*, A. C. Sprague (ed.), Phoenix edition (Chicago, 1965)

Davenant, W., *Gondibert*, D. F. Gladish (ed.) (Oxford, 1971)

Descartes, R., *Oeuvres*, C. Adam and P. Tannery (ed.), volume 1 (Paris, 1964)

Donne, J., *Poems*, H. J. C. Grierson (ed.), 2 volumes (Oxford, 1912)

Drayton, M., *Poems* (1619)

Dryden, J., *Poems*, J. Kinsley (ed.), 4 volumes (Oxford, 1958)

——*Of Dramatic Poesy and Other Critical Essays*, G. Watson (ed.), 2 volumes, Everyman's Library (1962)

Du Bartas, G., *Divine Weekes and Workes*, trans. J. Sylvester (1633)

Evelyn, J., *Sylva, or a Discourse of Forest-Trees* (1664)

——*Diary and Correspondence*, W. Bray (ed.) (1906)

——*Diary*, E. S. de Beer (ed.), 6 volumes (Oxford, 1955)

Ferguson, R., *The Interest of Reason in Religion* (1675)

Filmer, R., *Patriarcha and Other Political Works*, P. Laslett (ed.) (Oxford, 1949)

Fletcher, G., and P. Fletcher, *Poetical Works*, F. S. Boas (ed.), 2 volumes (Cambridge, 1908–9, 1970)

Glanvill, J., *Scepsis Scientifica, or, Confest Ignorance, the Way to Science* (1665)

——*Plus Ultra* (1668)

——*Philosophia Pia, Or, a Discourse of the Religious Temper, and Tendencies of the Experimental Philosophy* (1671)

——*Essays on Several Important Subjects in Philosophy and Religion* (1676)

——*The Vanity of Dogmatizing* (New York, 1931)

Greville, F., Lord Brooke, *Poems and Dramas*, G. Bullough (ed.), 2 volumes (Edinburgh, 1939)

Hales, J., *Works*, 3 volumes (Glasgow, 1765)

Hall, J., *Meditations and Vowes, Divine and Morall* (1605)

——*Epistles*, 3 volumes (1608)

Herbert, G., *Works*, F. E. Hutchinson (ed.) (Oxford, 1941)

Heyrick, T., *Miscellany Poems* (Cambridge, 1691)

Hobbes, T., *English Works*, W. Molesworth (ed.), 11 volumes (1839–45)

——*Leviathan*, M. Oakeshott (ed.) (Oxford, n.d.)

Hooke, R., *Micrographia* (1665)

——*Posthumous Works* R. Waller (ed.) (1705)

Hooker, R., *Works*, J. Keble (ed.), fourth edition, 3 volumes (Oxford, 1863)

Hyde, E., Earl of Clarendon, *The Life . . . Written by Himself*, 2 volumes (Oxford, 1857)

——*The History of the Great Rebellion*, R. Lockyer (ed.) (1967)

Jonson, B., *Works*, C. H. Herford, P. and E. Simpson (eds.), 11 volumes (Oxford, 1925–52)

Kennett, B., *The Lives and Characters of the Ancient Grecian Poets* (1697)

Laud, W., *Works*, 7 volumes (Oxford, 1847–60)

Lee, S., (ed.) *Elizabethan Sonnets*, 2 volumes (1904)

Locke, J., *An Essay Concerning Human Understanding*, J. W. Yolton (ed.), 2 volumes, Everyman's Library (1961)

Longinus, C., *Peri Hypsous, or Dionysius Longinus of the Height of Eloquence*, trans. J. Hall (1652)

——*On the Sublime*, trans. W. H. Fyfe, Loeb edition (1927)

Mackenzie, G., *Religio Stoici* (1665)

——*Works*, 2 volumes (Edinburgh, 1716–22)

Manilius, M., *The Five Books of M. Manilius, Containing a System of the Ancient Astronomy*, trans. T. Creech (1697)

———*Astronomica*, A. E. Housman (ed.), *editio minor* (Cambridge, 1932)

Manningham, T., *Two Discourses* (1681)

Marsh, R., *The Vanity and Danger of Modern Theories* (1699)

Marvell, A., *Poems and Letters*, H. M. Margoliouth (ed.), second edition, 2 volumes (Oxford, 1967)

Milton, J., *Works*, Columbia edition, F. A. Patterson and others (ed.s), 18 volumes (New York, 1931–8)

———*Complete Prose Works*, D. M. Wolfe and others (eds.) (New Haven, 1953–)

Montaigne, M. de., *Essais*, P. Villey (ed.), revised by V.-L. Saulnier (Paris, 1965)

O Hehir, B., *Expans'd Hieroglyphicks: A Critical Edition of Sir John Denham's Coopers Hill* (Berkeley, 1969)

Oldham, J., *Poems*, B. Dobrée (ed.), (1960)

Oldmixon, J., trans. *The Arts of Logick and Rhetorick* (1728)

Ovid, P. N., *The Art of Love and Other Poems*, Loeb edition, revised (1969)

Pindar, *Odes*, trans. G. West (1749)

———*Odes*, trans. C. M. Bowra, (Penguin books 1969)

Power, H., *Experimental Philosophy in Three Books* (1664)

Quintilian, M. F., *Institutio Oratoria*, trans. H. E. Butler, 4 volumes, Loeb edition (1920–2)

Sandys, G., *Ovid's Metamorphosis Englished* (1640)

Seneca, L. A., *Works*, trans. T. Lodge (1620)

———*Epistulae Morales*, trans. R. Gummere, 3 volumes, Loeb edition (1917–53)

Shelford, R., *Five Pious and Learned Discourses* (Cambridge, 1635)

Sidney, P., *Poems*, W. A. Ringler (ed.) (Oxford, 1962)

Simon, I., *Three Restoration Divines: Barrow, South, Tillotson: Selected Sermons*, volume 1 (Liege, 1967)

Simpson, W., *Philosophical Dialogues Concerning the Principles of Natural Bodies* (1677)

Smith, G. G., (ed.) *Elizabethan Critical Essays*, 2 volumes (Oxford, 1904)

South, R., *Forty Eight Sermons and Discourses on Several Subjects and Occasions*, third edition, 4 volumes (1715)

Spenser, E., *Minor Poems*, E. de Selincourt (ed.) (Oxford, 1910)

Spingarn, J. E. (ed.) *Critical Essays of the Seventeenth Century*, 3 volumes (Oxford, 1908–9)

Sprat, T., *The History of the Royal Society of London* (1667)

Tasso, T., *Jerusalem Delivered*, trans. E. Fairfax, with an introduction by R. Weiss (1962)

Virgil, P. M., *Virgil*, trans. H. R. Fairclough, 2 volumes, Loeb edition, revised (1950)

Waller, E., *Poems*, G. Thorn-Drury (ed.), 2 volumes (1905)

Wilkins, J., *An Essay Towards a Real Character and a Philosophical Language* (1668)

——*Of the Principles and Duties of Natural Religion* (1675)

Williams, A. M. (ed.) *Conversations at Little Gidding* (Cambridge,
1970)

Wilmot, J., Earl of Rochester, *Complete Poems*, D. M. Vieth (ed.)
(New Haven, 1968)

Woodford, S., *A Paraphrase upon the Psalms* (1667)

Works of Celebrated Authors, The, 2 volumes (1750)

Wotton, H., *Reliquiae Wottonianae* (1651)

——*Life and Letters*, L. P. Smith (ed.), 2 volumes (Oxford, 1907)

c)   SECONDARY SOURCES

This section does not include a check-list of Cowley-studies, for
which the reader is referred to the bibliography of Robert
Hinman's *Abraham Cowley's World of Order* (1960). I have, however,
listed the more significant or informative studies produced since
1960.

Aaron, R. I., *John Locke*, third edition (1971)

Adolph, R., *The Rise of Modern Prose Style* (Cambridge, Mass.,
1968)

Allen, D. C., 'Cowley's Pindar', MLN, 63 (1948), 184–5

——*Doubt's Boundless Sea: Scepticism and Faith in the Renaissance*
(Baltimore, 1964)

Alvarez, A., *The School of Donne* (1961)

Aston, T. (ed.) *Crisis in Europe, 1560–1660: Essays from 'Past and
Present'* (1965)

Bateson, G., *Steps to an Ecology of Mind* (1973)

Beaurline, L. A., 'Dudley North's Criticism of Metaphysical
Poetry', HLQ, 25 (1962), 299–313

Bethell, S. L., *The Cultural Revolution of the Seventeenth Century* (1951)

——'Gracián, Tesauro, and the Nature of Metaphysical Wit', *The Northern Miscellany of Literary Criticism*, 1 (1953), 19–40

Bowra, C. M., *Greek Lyric Poetry from Alcman to Simonides*, second edition (Oxford, 1961)

——*Pindar* (Oxford, 1964)

Broadbent, J. B., *Poetic Love* (1964)

Brower, R. A., 'Dryden's Epic Manner ånd Virgil', PMLA, 55 (1940), 119–38

——*Alexander Pope: The Poetry of Allusion* (Oxford, 1959)

Burtt, E. A., *The Metaphysical Foundations of Modern Science*, second edition (1967)

Bush, D., *English Literature in the Earlier Seventeenth Century, 1600–1660* (Oxford, 1945)

——*Science and English Poetry: A Historical Sketch, 1590–1950* (New York, 1950)

Butterfield, H., *The Origins of Modern Science, 1300–1800*, second edition (1957)

Calderhead, J. C., 'The Cherry and the Laurel: A Note on the Source of Lines in St. x of "The Garden"', NQ, 212 (1967), 337–9

Camps, W. A., *An Introduction to Virgil's Aeneid* (1969)

Chernaik, W. L., *The Poetry of Limitation: A Study of Edmund Waller* (New Haven, 1968)

Cochrane, R. C., 'Francis Bacon and the Architect of Fortune', *Studies in the Renaissance*, 5 (1958), 176–95

Colie, R., *Paradoxica Epidemica: The Renaissance Tradition of Paradox* (Princeton, 1966)

Coltman, I., *Private Men and Public Causes: Philosophy and Politics in the English Civil War* (1962)

Dijksterhuis, E. J., *Mechanization of the World Picture*, trans. C. Dikshoorn (Oxford, 1961)

Donahue, W. H., *The Dissolution of the Celestial Spheres, 1595–1650*, unpubl. Ph.D. diss., University of Cambridge, 1972

Elledge, S., 'Cowley's Ode "Of Wit" and Longinus on the Sublime', MLQ, 9 (1948), 185–98

Ellrodt, R., 'Scientific Curiosity and Metaphysical Poetry in the Seventeenth Century', MP, 61 (1964), 180–97

Ellul, J., *The Technological Society*, trans. J. Wilkinson (1965)

England, A. B., 'Swift's "An Elegy on Mr. Patrige" and Cowley's "On the Death of Mr. Crashaw"', NQ, 218 (1973), 412–3

Erskine-Hill, H., 'Rochester: Augustan or Explorer?', in *Renaissance and Modern Essays Presented to Vivian de Sola Pinto*, G. R. Hibbard (ed.) (1966), 51–64

Ferry, A. D., *Milton's Epic Voice: The Narrator in Paradise Lost* (Cambridge, Mass., 1963)

Fish, S. E. (ed.) *Seventeenth-Century Prose: Modern Essays in Criticism* (New York, 1971)

——*Self-Consuming Artifacts: The Experience of Seventeenth-Century Literature* (Berkeley, 1972)

Foucault, M., *The Order of Things: An Archaeology of the Human Sciences*, no translator's name (1970)

Fussner, F. S., *The Historical Revolution: English Historical Writing and Thought, 1580–1640* (1962)

Gay, P., *The Enlightenment: An Interpretation*, 2 volumes (1973)

Gerber, D. E., *A Bibliography of Pindar, 1513–1966* (Case Western Reserve University, 1969)

Gillispie, C. C., *The Edge of Objectivity: An Essay in the History of Scientific Ideas* (Princeton, 1960)

Goldstein, H. D., *Cowley and the 'Pindarick Madness'*, unpubl. Ph.D. diss., Northwestern University, 1960

——'Anglorum Pindarus: Model and Milieu', *Comparative Literature*, 17 (1965), 299–310

——'*Discordia Concors*, Decorum, and Cowley', *English Studies*, 49 (1968), 481–9

Gouhier, H., *La pensée métaphysique de Descartes* (Paris, 1962)

Greene, T., *The Descent from Heaven: A Study in Epic Continuity* (New Haven, 1963)

Griffin, D. H., *Satires Against Man: The Poems of Rochester* (Berkeley, 1973)

Grose, C., *Milton's Epic Process* (New Haven, 1973)

Hall, A. R., *The Scientific Revolution, 1500–1800* (1954)

Haller, W., *The Rise of Puritanism* (New York, 1938)

Hamilton, K. G., *The Two Harmonies: Poetry and Prose in the Seventeenth Century* (Oxford, 1963)

Harth, P., *Contexts of Dryden's Thought* (Chicago, 1968)

Hazard, P., *The European Mind, 1680–1715*, trans. J. L. May (1953)

Hill, C., *Puritanism and Revolution* (1958)

——*The Century of Revolution, 1603–1714* (Edinburgh, 1961)

——*Society and Puritanism in Pre-Revolutionary England* (1964)

——*Intellectual Origins of the English Revolution* (Oxford, 1965)

——*Reformation to Industrial Revolution* (1967)

——Milton and the English Revolution (1977)

Hinman, R. B., '"Truth Is Truest Poesy": The Influence of the New Philosophy on Abraham Cowley', ELH, 23 (1956), 194–203

——Abraham Cowley's World of Order (Cambridge, Mass., 1960)

Hoopes, R. G., Right Reason in the English Renaissance (Cambridge, Mass., 1962)

Hurd, R., Moral and Political Dialogues, sixth edition, 3 volumes (1788)

Jacquot, J., 'Sir Charles Cavendish and his Learned Friends', Annals of Science, 8 (1952), 13–27, 175–91

Jardine, L., Francis Bacon: Discovery and the Art of Discourse (Cambridge, 1974)

Johnson, S., Lives of the English Poets, G. B. Hill (ed.), 3 volumes (Oxford, 1905)

Jones, R. F., Ancients and Moderns, second edition (St Louis, 1961)

Jones, R. F., and others, The Seventeenth Century: Studies in the History of Thought and Literature from Bacon to Pope (Stanford, 1951)

Jordan, W. K., The Development of Religious Toleration in England, 1603–1640, reprinted (Gloucester, Mass., 1965)

Kamen, H., The Rise of Toleration (1967)

Kelliher, W. H., 'Crashaw's Contemporary Reputation', NQ, 213 (1968), 375

Kermode, F., 'The Date of Cowley's Davideis', RES, 25 (1949), 154–8

——Renaissance Essays (1971)

Klibansky, R., E. Panofsky, and F. Saxl, Saturn and Melancholy (1964)

Korshin, P., 'The Theoretical Bases of Cowley's Later Poetry', SP 66 (1969), 756–76

——(ed.) Studies in Change and Revolution: Aspects of English Intellectual History, 1640–1800 (Menston, 1972)

——From Concord to Dissent: Major Themes in English Poetic Theory, 1640–1700 (Menston, 1973)

Koyre, A., From the Closed World to the Infinite Universe (Baltimore, 1957)

Kristeller, P. O., Renaissance Thought (New York, 1961)

——Renaissance Thought II (New York, 1965)

——Eight Philosophers of the Italian Renaissance (1965)

Kuhn, T., The Structure of Scientific Revolutions, second edition (Chicago, 1970)

Labrousse, E. 'La méthode critique chez Pierre Bayle et l'Histoire', *Revue internationale de philosophie*, 11 (1957), 450–66
——*Pierre Bayle*, volume 1, *De pays de foix à la cité d'Erasme* (The Hague, 1963)
Land, S. K., *From Signs to Propositions: The Concept of Form in Eighteenth-Century Semantic Theory* (1974)
Langley, T. R., 'Cowley's Ode to Brutus: Royalist or Republican?', *Yearbook of English Studies*, 6 (1976), 41–52
——'Habemus Caesarem', unpubl. lectures
Leishman, J. B., *The Art of Marvell's Poetry* (1966)
——*The Monarch of Wit: An Analytical and Comparative Study of the Poetry of John Donne*, sixth edition (1967)
Lever, J. W., *The Elizabethan Love-Sonnet*, second edition (1966)
Loiseau, J., *Abraham Cowley: sa vie, son oeuvre* (Paris, 1931)
——*Abraham Cowley's Reputation in England* (Paris, 1931)
Madden, E. H., *Theories of Scientific Method: The Renaissance Through the Nineteenth Century* (Seattle, 1960)
Maddison, C., *Apollo and the Nine: A History of the Ode* (1960)
Martz, L., *The Poetry of Meditation*, revised edition (New Haven, 1962)
Mayo, T. F., *Epicurus in England, 1650–1725* (Dallas, 1934)
Mazzeo, J. A. (ed.) *Reason and the Imagination: Studies in the History of Ideas, 1600–1800* (New York, 1962)
——*Renaissance and Seventeenth-Century Studies* (New York, 1964)
——*Renaissance and Revolution: The Remaking of European Thought* (1967)
Miner, E. R., *The Metaphysical Mode from Donne to Cowley* (Princeton, 1969)
——*The Cavalier Mode from Jonson to Cotton* (Princeton, 1971)
——*The Restoration Mode from Milton to Dryden* (Princeton, 1974)
Mintz, S. I., *The Hunting of Leviathan* (Cambridge, 1962)
Momigliani, A., *Studies in Historiography* (1966)
Monk, S. H., *The Sublime: A Study of Critical Theories in Eighteenth Century England*, second edition (Michigan, 1960)
Nethercot, A. H., 'The Relation of Cowley's *Pindarics* to Pindar's *Odes*', MP, 19 (1921), 107–9
——'Abraham Cowley's *Essays*', JEGP, 29 (1930), 114–30
——'Concerning Cowley's Prose Style', PMLA, 46 (1931), 962–5
——*Abraham Cowley: The Muse's Hannibal* (Oxford, 1931)
——'Milton, Jonson, and the Young Cowley', MLN, 49 (1934), 158–62

Nicolson, M., *The Breaking of the Circle: Studies in the Effect of the 'New Science' Upon Seventeenth-Century Poetry* (Evanston, 1950)

Norwood, G., *Pindar* (Berkeley, 1945)

Orr, R. R., *Reason and Authority: The Thought of William Chillingworth* (Oxford, 1967)

Palmer, D. J., 'The Verse Epistle', *Stratford-upon-Avon Studies*, 11 (1970), 73–99

Piper, W. B., *The Heroic Couplet* (Cleveland, 1969)

Pocock, J. G. A., 'Time, History and Eschatology in the Thought of Thomas Hobbes', in *The Diversity of History: Essays in honour of Sir Herbert Butterfield*, J. H. Elliott and H. G. Koenigsberger (eds.) (1970), 151–98

Popkin, R. H., *The History of Scepticism from Erasmus to Descartes* (Assen, 1960)

Price, M., 'The Sublime Poem: Pictures and Powers', *Yale Review*, 58 (1969), 194–213

Pritchard, A., 'Puritan Charges Against Crashaw and Beaumont', TLS (1964), 578

——'Six Letters by Cowley', RES, n.s. 18 (1967), 253–63

Purver, M., *The Royal Society: Concept and Creation* (1967)

Quinn, K., *Virgil's Aeneid: A Critical Description* (1968)

Randall, J. H., *The School of Padua and the Emergence of Modern Science* (Padua, 1961)

Rawlinson, D., 'Cowley and the Current Status of Metaphysical Poetry', *Essays in Criticism*, 13 (1963), 323–40

Reif, P., 'The Textbook Tradition in Natural Philosophy, 1600–1650', JHI, 30 (1969), 17–32

Reuther, R. R., *Gregory of Nazianzanus: Rhetor and Philosopher* (Oxford, 1969)

Rice, E. F., *The Renaissance Idea of Wisdom* (Cambridge, Mass., 1958)

Richmond, H. M., *The School of Love: The Evolution of the Stuart Love Lyric* (Princeton, 1964)

Rivers, I., *The Poetry of Conservatism, 1600–1745* (Cambridge, 1973)

Rossi, P., *Francis Bacon: From Magic to Science*, trans. S. Rabinovitch (1968)

Rostvig, M.-S., *The Happy Man*, 2 volumes (Oslo, 1954–8)

Sayce, R. A., *The French Biblical Epic in the Seventeenth Century* (Oxford, 1955)

——*The Essays of Montaigne: A Critical Exploration* (1970)

Schuster, G. N., *The English Ode from Milton to Keats* (New York, 1940)

Selden, R., 'Hobbes and Late Metaphysical Poetry', JHI, 35 (1974), 197–210

Shafer, R., *The English Ode to 1660* (New York, 1918, 1966)

Sharp, R. L., *From Donne to Dryden: The Revolt Against Metaphysical Poetry* (Chapel Hill, 1940)

Smith, A. J., 'The Failure of Love: Love Lyrics after Donne', *Stratford-upon-Avon Studies*, 11 (1970), 41–71

——(ed.) *John Donne: Essays in Celebration* (1972)

Spencer, L. M. G., 'Johnson and Cowley', *The New Rambler*, June 1967, 18–32

Spragens, T. A., *The Politics of Motion: The World of Thomas Hobbes* (1973)

Steadman, J. M., *Milton and the Renaissance Hero* (Oxford, 1967)

——'Beyond Hercules: Bacon and the Scientist as Hero', *Studies in the Literary Imagination*, 4 (1971), 3–47

Stone, L., *The Causes of the English Revolution, 1529–1642* (1972)

Strier, R., 'Crashaw's Other Voice', SEL, 9 (1969), 135–51

Summers, J. H., *The Heirs of Donne and Jonson* (1970)

Taaffe, J. G., *Abraham Cowley* (New York, 1972)

Thompson, E. N. S., *The Seventeenth-Century English Essay* (New York, 1926)

Tillyard, E. M. W., *The English Epic and its Background* (1954)

Tracy, H. L., 'Thought-Sequence in the Ode', *The Phoenix*, 5 (1951), 108–18

Trevor-Roper, H. R., *Archbishop Laud, 1573–1645*, second edition (1962)

——'Clarendon', TLS (1975), 31–3

Trotter, W. D., *Abraham Cowley: An Interpretation of His Literary Procedures and Their Intellectual Context*, unpubl. Ph.D. diss., University of Cambridge, 1975

Tuve, R., *Elizabethan and Metaphysical Imagery* (Chicago, 1947)

Tuveson, E. L., *The Imagination as a Means of Grace* (Berkeley, 1960)

Van Leeuwen, H. G., *The Problem of Certainty in English Thought, 1630–1690* (The Hague, 1963)

Vickers, B., *Francis Bacon and Renaissance Prose* (Cambridge, 1968)

——(ed.) *Essential Articles for the Study of Francis Bacon* (1968)

Waldman, T., 'Origins of the Legal Doctrine of Reasonable Doubt', JHI, 20 (1959), 299–316

Wallace, J. M., '*Coopers Hill*: The Manifesto of Parliamentary Royalism, 1641', ELH, 41 (1974), 494–540

Wallerstein, R., *Studies in Seventeenth-Century Poetic* (Madison, 1950)

Walton, G., *The English Writings of Abraham Cowley*, unpubl. Ph. D. diss., University of Cambridge, 1940

——*Metaphysical to Augustan: Studies in Tone and Sensibility in the Seventeenth Century* (1955)

Warren, A., *Richard Crashaw: A Study in Baroque Sensibility* (1939)

Watzlawick, P., J. Beavin, and D. D. Jackson, *The Pragmatics of Human Communication* (New York, 1967)

Webster, C., 'Henry Power's Experimental Philosophy', *Ambix*, 14 (1967), 150–78

——(ed.) *The Intellectual Revolution of the Seventeenth Century* (1974)

——*The Great Instauration: Science, Medicine and Reform, 1626–1660* (1975)

Williamson, G., *The Proper Wit of Poetry* (1961)

——*A Reader's Guide to the Metaphysical Poets* (1968)

——*Seventeenth-Century Contexts*, revised edition (Chicago, 1969)

Willis, D. M., *The Mind and Art of Abraham Cowley*, unpubl. Ph.D. diss., Yale University, 1962

Wilson, P. B., *The Knowledge and Appreciation of Pindar in the Seventeenth and Eighteenth Centuries*, unpubl. Ph.D. diss., University of Oxford, 1974

Yates, F. A., *The Rosicrucian Enlightenment* (1972)

Yolton, J. W. (ed.) *John Locke: Problems and Perspectives* (Cambridge, 1969)

——*Locke and the Compass of Human Understanding* (Cambridge, 1970)

Index